THE ROGUE'S HANDBOOK

A CONCISE GUIDE TO CONDUCT
FOR THE ASPIRING GENTLEMAN ROGUE

JEFF METZGER

sourcebooks

Copyright © 2010 by Jeff Metzger

Cover and internal design © 2010 by Sourcebooks, Inc.

Cover design by The Book Designers

Cover image © Shutterstock.com

Internal images © Steven Wynn/iStockphoto.com; © 123foto/iStockphoto.com; © beetle8/iStockphoto.com; © Daniel Cooper/iStockphoto.com; © HultonArchive/iStockphoto.com; © Mikhail Bistrov/iStockphoto.com; © hande sengun/iStockphoto.com; © Kevin Russ/iStockphoto.com; © Luke Daniek/iStockphoto.com; © Sean Locke/iStockphoto.com; © ryan burke/iStockphoto.com; © Wolfgang Amri/iStockphoto.com; © Heather Wahl/iStockphoto.com; © Nancy Louie/iStockphoto.com; © Suprijono Suharjoto/iStockphoto.com; © Florea Marius Catalin/iStockphoto.com; © Sharon Dominick/iStockphoto.com; © Georgi Anchev/iStockphoto.com; © Stockphoto4u/iStockphoto.com; © Juanmonino/iStockphoto.com; © Dimitar Marinov/Fotolia.com; © Engine Images/Fotolia.com; © Lev Dolgatsjov/Fotolia.com; © diego cervo/Fotolia.com; © Ambrosede/Fotolia.com; © Maridav/Fotolia.com; © Pix by Marti/Fotolia.com; © imabase/Fotolia.com; © Amir Kaljikovic/Fotolia.com; © Anton Zabielskyi

Sourcebooks and the colophon are registered trademarks of Sourcebooks, Inc.

This publication is designed to provide accurate and authoritative information in regard to the subject matter covered. It is sold with the understanding that the publisher is not engaged in rendering legal, accounting, or other professional service. If legal advice or other expert assistance is required, the services of a competent professional person should be sought.—*From a Declaration of Principles Jointly Adopted by a Committee of the American Bar Association and a Committee of Publishers and Associations*

All brand names and product names used in this book are trademarks, registered trademarks, or trade names of their respective holders. Sourcebooks, Inc., is not associated with any product or vendor in this book.

Published by Sourcebooks, Inc.

P.O. Box 4410, Naperville, Illinois 60567-4410

(630) 961-3900

Fax: (630) 961-2168

www.sourcebooks.com

Library of Congress Cataloging-in-Publication data is on file with the publisher.

Printed and bound in the United States of America.

VP 10 9 8 7 6 5 4 3 2 1

When you go up to talk to her, man, I don't want you to be the guy in the PG-13 movie everyone's really hoping makes it happen. I want you to be like the guy in the rated-R movie, you know? The guy you're not sure whether or not you like yet. You're not sure where he's coming from, okay? You're a bad man, you're a bad man, you're a bad man!

—Trent Walker, *Swingers*

CONTENTS

INTRODUCTION

The Gentleman Rogue is a character who has fascinated us for centuries, persistently popping up in literature and cinema with a roguish smirk, causing proper gentlemen to frown with indignation and the bosoms of proper damsels to swell and flush. However, the Gentleman Rogue seems to be a vanishing species in the twenty-first century; whenever we see him, he is speaking to us from another time and place: a pirate, an outlaw, a Depression-era gangster. This may be a tragedy; however, the scarcity of G-Rogues in the twenty-first century only proves to make them more appealing on the rare occasion that we encounter them. (Take Russian billionaire Mikhail Prokhorov, for example. How refreshing is it in this day and age to see a business tycoon who is not a crusty old killjoy, but rather a much younger, much richer version of Hugh Hefner?) Although the very fact that the Gentleman Rogue is an anachronism may account for a portion of our initial attraction to him, there are many other elements to his singular nature that contribute to the undeniable love/hate magnetism that he inspires in us. He may not be a nice person; he may not even be a fundamentally decent person; he is certainly not a very proper person. But no one can deny that he is interesting, providing a splash of color among the mass of men leading lives of quiet desperation. Whether or not the Gentleman Rogue is praiseworthy or a useful member of society is not at issue here and will neither be studied, questioned, nor discussed. I do not submit that the Gentleman Rogue is commendable, but I do submit that he is fascinating.

Here we shall endeavor to study such G-Rogue All-Stars as Rhett Butler, James Bond, Indiana Jones, Captain Jack Sparrow, and a fictional character we will refer to simply as "G-Rogue," and try to learn exactly what it is about them that causes men to clench their fists and induces women to swoon. If your wish is to reinvent yourself as someone who leaves clenched fists and flushed, heaving bosoms in your wake, read on carefully.

Era: Late twelfth-century England.

Appearance: Rugged G-Rogue. Not dressed with the knightly pomp of his Norman counterparts (chain mail, lavish coats of arms, thick luxurious capes, etc.). Rather, he is attired like a rugged outdoorsman: Lincoln green clothes, tall boots, feathered woodsman hat, a longbow, quiver of arrows, and sword. In the right light, he can also resemble an anthropomorphic cartoon fox.

Habitat: Once upon a time, Robin could be found in his stately castle. After it was seized by the tyrannous government, he could be found in the much more meager surroundings of Sherwood Forest. There he would enjoy an eight-year-old boy's paradise, climbing trees, swinging from vines, repeatedly falling into streams, ambushing, pillaging, and plundering. On the downside, there was no wine cellar in the forest and not a chamber pot for miles.

Women: Robin was a Saxon, and he was hot for a Norman girl. In twelfth-century England, that was nothing short of Jungle Fever. Marian haughtily despises him at first, and he responds to her attitude with mocking amusement. ("Tsk tsk tsk, what a pity your manners don't match your looks, Your Highness!") Whether by virtue of Robin's impertinent charm, or due to a personal revelation regarding class struggle, she suddenly realizes she has a thing for Saxon guys. Robin's boldness of romantic attack is impressive—not only does he steal Marian away from a rival suitor, but he goes so far as to sneak into the rival's castle to woo her under his very nose.

Turn-ons: Norman chicks, social justice, archery, mutton.

Turn-offs: Usurpers, treachery, a regressive income tax.

Quote: Lovely Lass [shocked and offended]: "Why, you speak treason!" Robin Hood [matter-of-factly]: "Fluently."

G-Rogue Credentials: "He's a notorious troublemaker." Robin has his castle and possessions seized for instigating class warfare, and he cheerfully turns outlaw and takes to the forest. "He's an impudent, reckless rogue who goes around the shires stirring up the Saxons against authority." He is under death sentence, yet confidently walks into the castle of his would-be executioner. He's the best archer in England, and a maestro at swordplay as well. He pioneers the concept of wealth redistribution before it caught on in Europe. He is a "King of Outlaws and Prince of Good Fellows," and meets both good fortune and ill with mirth and raucous laughter. "He is different from anyone I've ever known. He's brave, and he's reckless..." And he steals her away from her rival suitor, and gives him a sword to the stomach for good measure.

G-ROGUE PROFILE:
CAPTAIN JACK SPARROW

Era: Seventeenth-century Caribbean.

Appearance: Rugged G-Rogue. Puffy pirate shirt, tri-cornered hat. Always carrying his "effects," which include a sword and pistol. Long, tangled hair, braided goatee, a plethora of gold teeth. Questionable personal hygiene. Lots and lots of eye makeup.

Habitat: At the helm of the Black Pearl sailing across the Caribbean, in any sort of cell or brig, on the gallows, stranded on a desert island with a gigantic cache of rum, recruiting sailors or incurring female wrath in seedy Tortuga, battling supernatural pirates or upstart blacksmiths, jumping, diving, or swinging across the screen, in Davy Jones's Locker.

Women: He endures endless slaps at the hands of women he may or may not have wronged or offended, claiming that some of them he deserved and some he did not. He is very talented at the double entendre and extended sexual metaphor ("Granted, it tends to list to port, and has been on occasion known to frighten young women. But I promise you, you will not be disappointed."). The Lovely Lass Elizabeth's bosom is constantly flushed and heaving in his presence, but it is impossible to determine if this condition is caused by Jack's roguishness or by her rather constrictive corset.

THE ROGUE'S HANDBOOK

Turn-ons: *The Black Pearl*, rum, Tortuga strumpets, mascara, the word "Captain."

Turn-offs: Enormous aquatic beasties, fair fights, supernatural antagonists, guys in wigs.

Quote: "I'm dishonest, and a dishonest man you can always trust to be dishonest. Honestly."

G-Rogue Credentials: Thoroughly inscrutable, no one ever has any idea what Jack Sparrow's motivation is, what is going through his head at any given moment, or even whose side he's on. He behaves reprehensibly and duplicitous much of the time, but then he turns around and exhibits inexplicable honor. He saves a Lovely Lass from drowning when he knew it would cause him trouble; he turns around to help Will and Elizabeth with the beastie when he had already safely escaped; he cedes immortality to save the life of a lovelorn wannabe he doesn't even like very much. A great lover of rum, he grows despondent at its disappearance. Garners slaps from the ladies at a remarkable frequency. His speech is preposterously verbose, accented, disdainful, yet courteous: "I have no sympathy for any of you feculent maggots and no more patience to pretend otherwise. Gentlemen, I wash my hands of this weirdness."

1

"GENTLEMAN ROGUE" DEFINED

"**G**entleman Rogue" is obviously an oxymoron, a contradiction in terms. A gentleman is not a rogue, and a rogue is certainly not a gentleman. Combining these two diametric definitions into a single individual seems like an exercise in

G-Rogue Walt Whitman was writing about his "tremulous love-flesh" a century before anybody knew what the hell he was talking about.

futility. But the Gentleman Rogue is a mystery of many parts—as Walt Whitman (who somehow managed to be a G-Rogue despite the fact that he was probably gay or bisexual) wrote:

"Do I contradict myself? Very well, then, I contradict myself, (I am large, I contain multitudes.)"

Before attempting a half-baked venture at characterizing this enigma, let us first define the parts of the whole.

gen-tle-man, *noun*. 1. a man of noble or gentle birth; 2. a man who combines gentle birth or rank with chivalrous qualities; 3. a man whose conduct conforms to a high standard of propriety or correct behavior.

—*Merriam-Webster's Dictionary*

rogue, *noun*. 1. an unprincipled, deceitful, and unreliable person; a scoundrel or rascal; 2. one who is playfully mischievous; a scamp; 3. an organism, especially a plant, that shows an undesirable variation from a standard.

—*American Heritage Dictionary*

The Gentleman Rogue is a combination of these definitions, although there is no system or rule concerning how they are to be mixed or in what percentages to amalgamate. All of these definitions can be true of the G-Rogue... though in their own fashion. Let's look closer at each one.

"A man of noble birth."

The G-Rogue very often appears to us as "a prince in rogue's clothing." This could include men of noble birth who choose a more plebeian existence (Robin Hood, Athos) or men who have been brought up to think they are common but who secretly have blue blood running through their veins (Lone Starr from *Spaceballs*). This definition also applies to our Gentleman Rogues who actually are members of the aristocracy but are simply a trifle roguish (Lord Byron, Winston

Aristocratic G-Rogue Lord Byron was "mad, bad, and dangerous to know."

Churchill, Count Almásy of *The English Patient*) or even flat-out devilish (Marquis de Sade). In many cases the Gentleman Rogue is not necessarily of patrician blood *per se,* but he nearly always comports himself with an air of nobility, as is most clearly evidenced by his language.

"Chivalrous qualities."

The Gentleman Rogue's interaction with the fair sex is obviously one of his most distinguishing characteristics and thus warrants close study. The G-Rogue will very often express himself as a knight in shining armor in manners and speech: addressing women with courtesy and respect; bowing and holding open doors; and, perhaps most importantly, coming to the aid of damsels in distress. However, before you can blink your eye, the G-Rogue will do or say something outrageously divergent from the standard codes of chivalry. James Bond—ever the tuxedoed and gallant British gentleman—made a living on inappropriate comments delivered to fair maidens betwixt moments of perfect chivalry. John Dillinger famously berated one of his confederates for cursing in

Sir Lancelot was nothing if not chivalrous, yet he stole his boss's wife—pretty solid G-Rogue credentials.

the presence of a lady (hostage) during the course of a crime spree. In *The Philadelphia Story*, Jimmy Stewart caustically says to Cary Grant, "Always the gentleman, eh?" Grant's C. K. Dexter Haven pauses for a moment of consideration, then replies, "Except on occasion." The Gentleman Rogue is inevitably the Mercurial Chevalier—always the paragon of chivalry… except on occasion.

"A man whose conduct conforms to a high standard of propriety or correct behavior."

This is perhaps the one unadulterated true characteristic of a Gentleman Rogue. His conduct always conforms to a very strict code. BUT—the code is his own and does not conform to society's conventional standards.

Social mores may come and go as time and place changes, but the G-Rogue's own code is eternal and intransient. Like Nietzsche's Superman, he is beyond good and evil—he creates his own moral universe.

Jack Tanner in *Man and Superman* enthusiastically commends a young lady for the bravery of thumbing her nose at social conventions by proudly bearing a child out of wedlock (until he finds that she is secretly married and grossly offended by his presumption). No doubt thirteenth-century English high society did not consider Robin Hood's habit of robbing his aristocratic peers as socially acceptable, though said behavior was absolutely correct and requisite in his own moral universe. Captain Jack Sparrow's personal code is almost entirely inscrutable, but one does get the feeling that all of his actions do conform to some kind of strange system of buccaneer ethics.

While the G-Rogue may seemingly be the pinnacle of non-conformity, he conforms strictly and almost stubbornly to his own code of behavior.

"Unprincipled, deceitful, and unreliable."

The Gentleman Rogue is seldom intentionally deceitful, as this runs contrary to almost any interpretation of chivalry. However, he is a contradiction by definition and as such eternally unreliable—unless you understand the singular code of behavior by which he lives. The G-Rogue may frequently be considered unprincipled, but only because his principles diverge from the established social norms.

A favorite activity of the Gentleman Rogue is to steal women away from passionless betrothals and relationships.

G-ROGUE QUOTE:

"I'm dishonest, and a dishonest man you can always trust to be dishonest. Honestly."

—Captain Jack Sparrow, *Pirates of the Caribbean*

Does he owe a greater allegiance to the social institution of engagement, or to the sacred calling of Love with a capital "L" and the future happiness of all parties concerned? The Gentleman Rogue is never afraid to fairly and squarely steal a fair maiden away from another suitor. (This fundamental attribute will be explored in more detail in a subsequent section.) To some, this character trait would be considered profoundly unprincipled.

"One who is playfully mischievous."

This is the second absolute characteristic of a textbook Gentleman Rogue. He is always playful, often in spite of the circumstances. Even when Rhett Butler's prospects of winning over Scarlett seemed bleakest, he always had an impertinent joke and a roguish grin. James Bond never lacked a suggestive quip, even when Death by Femme Fatale seemed imminent. A resilient sense of humor, preferably laced with improprieties and innuendo, is essential to the G-Rogue. After all, as Gentleman Rogue Oliver Goldsmith teaches us, "Girls like to be played with, and rumpled a little too, sometimes."

"An undesirable deviation from the standard."

The masses do not desire a Gentleman Rogue to be in their midst; the herd fears nonconformity. Who can blame them, really? The G-Rogue thumbs his nose at their conventions; he makes them appear bland and colorless; he steals their women. The black sheep is an undesirable deviation from the standard, because he threatens the desirability of the standard. And so much more does the herd fear a wolf in its midst.

MORE THAN THE SUM

Now we understand the parts of the whole. But the Gentleman Rogue is the very definition of gestalt. He blends the qualities of refinement with those of scandal in no particular combination, alchemically producing a creature that is not quite gentleman, not quite rogue, but all man.

Qualities of a Gentleman Rogue...

1. An air of nobility
2. A (perhaps surprising) chivalrous streak
3. An unbendable personal code of ethics (often at odds with society's)

4. Scandalous and regarded as unprincipled

5. A playfully mischievous sense of humor

6. Nonconformity

7. Well spoken

8. An intriguing (if not attractive) appearance

9. Independent

10. Daring

11. Intelligent

12. Courteous

13. Confident

14. Mysterious

15. Did we mention scandalous?

WINSTON CHURCHILL

Era: Twentieth-century United Kingdom.

Appearance: Refined G-Rogue. Three-piece suits, pocket watches, top hats. A face bearing the mark of a lifetime of epicurean indulgences. Often seen with a cocktail, always seen with a Cuban cigar.

Habitat: Most comfortable on battlefields, or drinking champagne in great excess at his country estate. Also could be found in various castles, at Parliament, or chilling with the The Big Three.

Women: Never bashful about using his wit and sarcasm to inspire blushing indignation from the ladies.

Churchill: "Madam, would you sleep with me for five million pounds?"

Lovely Lass: "My goodness, Mr. Churchill…Well, I suppose…we would have to discuss terms, of course."

Churchill: "Would you sleep with me for five pounds?"

Lovely Lass: "Mr. Churchill, what kind of woman do you think I am?!"

Churchill: "Madam, we've already established that. Now we are haggling about the price."

Turn-ons: Cigars, war, champagne, scotch, brandy.

Turn-offs: Nazis, Communists, teetotalers.

Quote: Indignant Gentleman: "At Eton they taught us to wash our hands after using the toilet."

Churchill: "At Harrow they taught us not to piss on our hands."

G-Rogue Credentials: Son of a lord, grandson of a duke, born in a palace. Ever courteous in speech and manner, even while using his wit for humiliation purposes. When he escaped from a POW camp in South Africa, he left a polite note apologizing for departing in such an unmannerly fashion. Overwhelming sense of confidence, as this quote regarding the possibility of dying on the battlefield exhibits: "I do not believe the gods would create so potent a being as myself for so prosaic an ending." During World War I, he displayed great courage by requesting to go to the front instead of working from the safety of battalion headquarters... but it turned out that alcohol was permitted in the trenches, but not at battalion headquarters. During World War II, he had his flight suit and oxygen mask customized to allow him to smoke cigars while wearing it. His cigar consumption in two days was the equivalent of one week's salary for his manservant.

G-ROGUE PROFILE:
HAN SOLO

Era: A long time ago, in a galaxy far, far away.

Appearance: Rugged G-Rogue. Black and white clothes: tunic unbuttoned at the top, vest, boots, packing a laser gun in a low-slung holster. Shaggy hair, sardonic smirk. Occasionally disguised as a Storm Trooper.

Habitat: Flying with a Sasquatch through the galaxy on smuggling missions or rescue missions, blowing away bounty hunters in seedy bars, hanging morosely on Jabba the Hut's wall, cavorting with Muppets.

Women: Has the hots for a princess, a girl well above his station. He is at turns sarcastic, impertinent, and boldly sexual with her. She responds with undisguised indignation and borderline disgust. But her will is eventually no match for his roguish ways. "You like me because I'm a scoundrel. There aren't enough scoundrels in your life." "I happen to like nice men." "I'm a nice man." "No, you're not. You're—" [They kiss with nervous passion, illustrating that she doesn't like nice men at all, but rather gentlemen rogues.]

Turn-ons: Girls in metal bikinis, extremely hirsute menservants, souped-up pieces of junk that can go really fast.

Turn-offs: Authority, morbidly obese frog-eating gangsters, carbonite, whiny kids going on and on about mystic philosophy.

Quote: Lovely Lass: "Let go, please."

Han Solo: "Don't get excited."

Lovely Lass: "Captain, being held by you isn't quite enough to get me excited."

Han Solo: "Sorry sweetheart. I haven't got time for anything else."

G-Rogue Credentials: A smuggler and a mercenary, Han Solo is essentially an intergalactic pirate. He seems extremely cynical and sarcastic, and makes it very clear that he is helping strictly for financial gain. ("I ain't in it for your revolution, and I'm not in this for you, princess. I expect to be well paid. I'm in it for the money.") But his actions belie his words, and he repeatedly saves the day at great personal risk when there is nothing in it for him. He won his spaceship in a card game. He has a price on his head, and bounty hunters are chasing him all over the galaxy. He is constantly causing Leia to blush with fury and indignation, but that blush of fury transitions into a blush of passion. His confidence knew she would come around; when she finally admits that she loves him, he replies, "I know."

SPEECH

The Gentleman Rogue says "my dear" as much as humanly possible.

If you take away nothing else away from this lesson, memorize the above proverb and you will make, at worst, a passable Gentleman Rogue. The phrase "my dear" immediately suggests intimacy and creates a sexual tension where none may have previously existed. In addition, it is an anachronistic address seldom heard in the twenty-first century, and the use of it will no doubt evoke the memory of a bygone era of chivalry, setting the G-Rogue apart from rival suitors who employ more pedestrian forms of speech (or, God forbid, colloquial postmodern addresses such as "girl" or "baby"). For example:

Rival Suitor: "Girl, you look hot tonight."

G-Rogue: "My dear, you are the very picture of loveliness."

"My dear" is not, however, restricted to the ritual of flirtation. While the gentleman may utilize this intimate address strictly to endear himself to a young lady, the G-Rogue takes great delight in juxtaposing it with a roguish message. Of course, *Gone with the Wind* provides us with the textbook example:

Scarlett O'Hara: "Where will I go, what will I do?"

Rhett Butler: "Frankly, my dear, I don't give a damn."

Frankly, my dear, Rhett Butler is one of the greatest G-Rogues of all time.

Or note the intimate impertinence of Sean Connery's 007 in *Thunderball*:

James Bond: "My dear girl, don't flatter yourself. What I did this evening was for King and country. You don't think it gave me any pleasure, do you?"

Those skilled in advanced gentleman roguery may wish to underscore their culture and erudition by using foreign-language "my dear" equivalents, such as "*ma cherie*" or "*mi querida.*"

He Might Be a G-Rogue if He Says...

1. My dear
2. I beg your pardon?
3. One (used as an indefinite pronoun)
4. Quite (used as a complete sentence)
5. How do you do?
6. Charming
7. Ciao
8. Sir
9. Madam
10. Be that as it may
11. After you
12. Nevertheless
13. Correct usage of "who" and "whom"
14. I don't always drink beer, but when I do, I prefer Dos Equis

"Your abode is quite charming, my dear, but with whom must one speak in order to get a cocktail?"

He is Not a G-Rogue if He Says...

1. Fuckin' (followed by any word [e.g., "fuckin' wasted," "fuckin' crazy," etc.])

2. Dude

3. Yo

4. Ain't

5. Bitch

6. Coarse synonyms for parts of the anatomy

7. Diss

8. Brewski
9. Anti-gay epithets
10. Baby Momma
11. I reckon
12. Booty
13. Bong
14. Gimme a Natty Light

Famous G-Rogue Quotes

"Fuckin' A, dude, I reckon I need another brewski!"

1. "There's a shortage of perfect breasts in the world; it would be a pity to damage yours."

   —Westley, *The Princess Bride*

2. "I have a great mind to believe in Christianity for the mere pleasure of fancying I may be damned."—Lord Byron

3. "Shaken, not stirred."—James Bond

4. "I'm the only cause I'm interested in."—Rick Blaine, *Casablanca*

5. "You like me because I'm a scoundrel. There aren't enough scoundrels in your life."—Han Solo, *The Empire Strikes Back*

6. "He has all the virtues I dislike and none of the vices I admire."—Winston Churchill

7. "I have taken more out of alcohol than alcohol has taken out of me."—Winston Churchill

8. "I'm dishonest, and a dishonest man you can always trust to be dishonest. Honestly."—Captain Jack Sparrow, *Pirates of the Caribbean: The Curse of the Black Pearl*

9. "Don't flatter yourself, I'm not a marrying man."—Rhett Butler, *Gone with the Wind*

10. "Frankly, my dear, I don't give a damn."—Rhett Butler, *Gone with the Wind*

KEYS TO THE G-ROGUE'S SPEECH

It is of the utmost importance that the aspiring Gentleman Rogue never underestimates the power of speech, and he must understand all the manifold messages a single sentence may convey. After the relating of a brief anecdote, his listener will make ten thousand assumptions, passing judgment on the speaker's intelligence, education, panache, culture, humor, social status, and sexual magnetism. Thus, a Gentleman

Rogue must be articulate and must express himself well. Message or humor notwithstanding, one may usually identify a G-Rogue if his *manner* of speaking is consistent with the following guidelines.

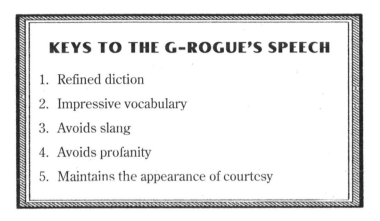

KEYS TO THE G-ROGUE'S SPEECH

1. Refined diction
2. Impressive vocabulary
3. Avoids slang
4. Avoids profanity
5. Maintains the appearance of courtesy

1. Refined Diction

The Gentleman Rogue speaks with clarity, with cadence, and with confidence. Even if he is speaking drivel, the G-Rogue appears to be intelligent and refined, because the balderdash is flowing from his mouth with great beauty. Listeners will gauge his perspicacity, education, and social status based on his enunciation, pronunciation, and rhythm.

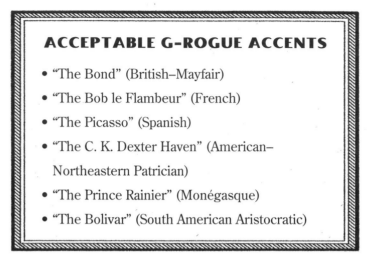

ACCEPTABLE G-ROGUE ACCENTS

- "The Bond" (British–Mayfair)
- "The Bob le Flambeur" (French)
- "The Picasso" (Spanish)
- "The C. K. Dexter Haven" (American–
  Northeastern Patrician)
- "The Prince Rainier" (Monégasque)
- "The Bolivar" (South American Aristocratic)

Classical Gentleman Rogue Theory may suggest that accents are to be avoided. However, it is rather the type of accent that must be considered, specifically as it applies to social status. European accents are especially desirable, as they often (justly or unjustly) evoke culture, sophistication, and experience. Working-class accents are typically to be avoided, whether they hail from the Bronx, East L.A., or the East End of London. (There are always exceptions, however, and we know very well that one of the common G-Rogue archetypes is the "prince in rogue's clothing.")

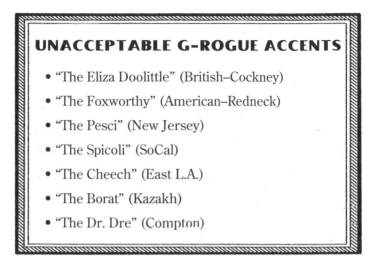

UNACCEPTABLE G-ROGUE ACCENTS

- "The Eliza Doolittle" (British–Cockney)
- "The Foxworthy" (American–Redneck)
- "The Pesci" (New Jersey)
- "The Spicoli" (SoCal)
- "The Cheech" (East L.A.)
- "The Borat" (Kazakh)
- "The Dr. Dre" (Compton)

In an effort to increase his G-Rogue Quotient, the man behind C. K. Dexter Haven changed his name as well as his accent.

2. Impressive Vocabulary

An impressive vocabulary is clear evidence of intelligence and erudition, requisite qualities of a Gentleman Rogue. The G-Rogue takes great pleasure in his language, substituting sesquipedalian synonyms for common monosyllabic words in order to liven up his speech and throw his superior learning in the face of the world. His word choice also succeeds in making him unique, setting him apart from the hoi polloi with their omnipresent slang and unimaginative eighth-grade phrases.

It should be noted that the aspiring Gentleman Rogue need not be a genius in order to expand his vocabulary and appear to be a beaconing tower of learning. The simple memorization of twenty or thirty impressive words or charmingly antiquated phrases will serve to increase one's perceived perspicacity by leaps and bounds (although, of course, this is no substitute for a more thorough education).

JOE SIX-PACK => G-ROGUE TRANSLATOR

Joe Six-Pack	G-Rogue
Bitches	Ladies
Baby	My dear
Fuckin'	Very, rather, or quite
Huh?	I beg your pardon?
Fag	Dandy
Phat	Chic
'Sup?	How do you do?
My gat	My manservant's pistol

Consider the paired remarks below and decide for yourself which are more impressive:

Joe Six-Pack: "You callin' me a liar, man?"
G-Rogue: "Sir, are you impugning my veracity?"

Joe Six-Pack: "What's up? Why you don't wanna drink?"

G-Rogue: "Come now, there's nothing more salubrious than a bibulous libation."

Joe Six-Pack: "Baby, you don't understand; things have been fucked up lately."

G-Rogue: "My dear, you can't fathom the viscosity of my present quagmire."

Joe Six-Pack: "Dude, I got laid last night."

G-Rogue: "Yes, *mon ami,* I suppose I was fortunate enough to have engaged in a memorable amorous liaison yesterday evening."

Joe Six-Pack: "Man, I was fuckin' wasted last night. Crazy shit musta happened, but I don't remember jack."

G-Rogue: "I fear I imbibed with intemperance last evening. My memory fails me, but misadventures no doubt transpired."

Joe Six-Pack: "Girl, you crazy!"

G-Rogue: "Madam, you seem to be suffering from a nervous affliction of some sort."

Joe Six-Pack: "Get a fuckin' move on, man! The party is already bumpin'!"

G-Rogue: "The soiree is approaching a crescendo; get thee hither, posthaste!"

3. Avoids Slang

The Gentleman Rogue eschews slang, just as he eschews all passing trends in general. He does not "go with the flow"; remember—by definition, he exhibits a deviation from the standard. Slang represents a transient fancy, something popular with the masses for a brief period.

The Gentleman Rogue is much more likely to scoff at the latest fashions in speech, dress, or custom rather than adapt to them. Those who employ excessive slang (whether they be urban colloquialisms or bucolic expressions) will often be

NON–G-ROGUE QUOTE:

"What the dilly, yo?"

judged (fairly or unfairly) as deficient in intellect, education, culture, social status, or at the very least, originality.

This is not to say that every G-Rogue must speak in New England prep school parlance rather than the local vernacular. A Gentleman Rogue may exist in any time and place, and his speech may reflect that fact; however, he will typically not adopt new idioms as they come into fashion.

4. Avoids Profanity

The Gentleman Rogue typically avoids profanities in everyday speech, as frequent usage of such words suggests an association with the lower classes or a lack of education. Occasional use of profanity, however, is not only permitted of a Gentleman Rogue but is also perhaps essential to his purpose.

NON—G-ROGUE QUOTE:

"Bitches ain't shit but hoes and tricks."

—Snoop Dogg, from Dr. Dre's "Bitches Ain't Shit"

Profane words or remarks have a specific function: to shock or to express extreme emphasis. In this day and age, unfortunately, one notices the increasing prevalence of profanity in everyday speech among the hoi polloi. If profane words are used in situations where no emphasis is necessary, they lose all shock value and are absolutely useless as a social tool—and the only thing they emphasize is a lack of refinement.

However, if a man who seldom curses unexpectedly inserts a "fuck" or a "goddamn" into his otherwise refined remarks, the room will no doubt go silent, and one may observe among his audience clenched fists or faces flushed with indignation. The G-Rogue, once again, owns the room.

5. Maintains the Appearance of Courtesy

As seen in the previous scenario, the Gentleman Rogue always comports himself with perfect courtesy in speech and manner, even in the face of discourtesy. Courtesy was one of the virtues of the chivalric knight in the Middle Ages, and the G-Rogue exhibits the characteristic in much the same fashion.

Now, it is a simple and indistinguishing task to behave courteously with friends and with ladies. But what sets the

G-Rogue apart from the throng is his penchant for choosing civil words when speaking with adversaries or when confronted with antagonism. He addresses his enemies as sir or madam and ornaments his disdain with politeness and pleasantries. Consider G-Rogue Winston Churchill:

Although he had perhaps the most acerbic wit of the twentieth century, Sir Winston always maintained a patina of courteous language.

Antagonist: "You, sir, are drunk!"

Churchill: "Yes, but you, madam, are ugly—and I shall be sober in the morning."

Antagonist: "If you were my husband, I would feed you poison!"

Churchill: "If you were my wife, madam, I would take it."

The G-Rogue's indomitable sense of courtesy will be further explored in a subsequent section. If you object, my dear sir, you may go fuck yourself.

SPEECH CASE STUDIES

Now that we have thoroughly studied all of the nuances of the G-Rogue's speech, let us consider some real situations and how the always-proper Fancy Lad, the coarse Joe Six-Pack, and the ever-suave Gentleman Rogue verbally respond to the following scenarios. (Note the clear superiority of the G-Rogue's replies.)

Situation #1

Our protagonist in question is at a wedding reception, and he is one of the tuxedoed groomsmen. The girl at his side is the maid of honor and the most ravishing female in the expansive, crowded room. The tuxedoed man and Ravishing Maid of Honor are standing near their table, sipping wine, chatting quietly and privately, and laughing a bit. They have stepped away from the wedding party's table because the best man has been making bold advances on Ravishing Maid of Honor, much to the wonder and chagrin of the tuxedoed man. As the band strikes up the first slow song of the evening, the best man bounces up behind the Ravishing Maid of Honor and addresses her with a suggestive grin: "So...when does the best man get to dance with the maid of honor, eh?"

How does the tuxedoed man respond?

The Fancy Lad's Response

[Silently observes Ravishing Maid of Honor as she struggles for a response and looks to him for help; he shrugs helplessly, so she reluctantly turns to the best man and says, "Now is fine, I suppose." He bows with perfect courtesy as the two of them walk to the dance floor.]

Result: Ravishing Maid of Honor goes home with the best man that night. Fancy Lad goes home alone, attempts to console himself with a bottle of cognac and the poetry of Alfred, Lord Tennyson.

Joe Six-Pack's Response

[Furrowing his prominent brow with rage and jabbing his finger in the best man's chest.] "What the fuck, asshole? Get your own fuckin' date!" [He roughly takes Ravishing Maid of Honor by the wrist and stomps to the dance floor.]

Result: Ravishing Maid of Honor dances with Joe

Six-Pack but gazes over his shoulder with boredom. She soon claims that she has a headache and excuses herself early from the reception. Joe Six-Pack consoles himself with excessive servings of mass-produced domestic light beer and then later initiates a fisticuff with a fellow troglodyte.

The G-Rogue's Response

[Speaking in a clear tone, with perfect civility.] "After she dances with her date. Now sit the *fuck* down, sir. And please watch our wine." [He hands the stunned best man two glasses

of wine, then turns to the Ravishing Maid of Honor.] "My dear," he says, extending his hand toward the dance floor in invitation. Smiling, she proceeds to the dance floor, bosom flushed and heaving. He follows.

Result: "Yes, *mon ami,* I suppose I was fortunate enough to have engaged in a memorable amorous liaison yesterday evening."

Situation #2

Our casually well-groomed protagonist walks into a high-end pet store with an impeccably groomed and obediently leashed Rhodesian Ridgeback. After three or four minutes of shopping, he finds himself standing at a register in front of the cashier, who happens to be a ravishing young dog lover. He looks into her eyes as he sets his purchases down. "Special occasion?" Ravishing Dog Lover asks. "Yes," our protagonist replies, "for her birthday I usually give her a new toy, a great big bone, and half a beer." The Ravishing Dog Lover hasn't broken eye contact as she's been scanning the items, and now she gives the protagonist a mischievous grin. "Is that what you give all your lady friends for their birthdays?"

How does the owner of the Ridgeback respond?

The Fancy Lad's Response

[Blushes crimson, breaks eye contact, stammers incoherently for a few seconds.] "Oh...oh, no, ma'am...I generally have flowers delivered." [He gives the leash a jerk, hastily says, "Come, Queenie," and hurries out the door before that tart can say something beastly again.]

Result: Ravishing Dog Lover shrugs her shoulders and continues to daydream about the roguish customer who will one day walk in and sweep her off her feet.

Joe Six-Pack's Response

[Furrows his prominent brow in apparent confusion.] "Huh?" [Shakes his head vigorously to clear his mind of the riddle.] "Anyways, what time you get off, babe? Wanna chill later?"

Result: Ravishing Dog Lover looks down sadly at the Ridgeback. "You understood that, didn't you, boy? Next in line—"

The G-Rogue's Response

[Holds eye contact for a long, smirking moment before speaking.] "Something like that, my dear. I give them a new toy and quite a prodigious bone...but I let them have a full beer."

Result: Ravishing Dog Lover looks down at her hands and laughs nervously, bosom flushed and heaving under her uniform polo shirt. Then she looks back up at the still silently smirking G-Rogue with a shy smile. "You know, today's my birthday, too..."

Situation #3

Our protagonist is wearing a black suit and tie. Although the funeral was understandably funereal, several hours of social lubrication at the wake has caused everyone's spirits to lift. He is talking to a ravishing young mourner clad in an elegant black dress, with whom he has been drinking pinot noir for the past two hours. "When I die," she says, "you should carry out the old Jewish tradition and dig a hole, put me in it, then fill it up yourself."

How does the black-suited mourner respond?

The Fancy Lad's Response

[Glancing morosely at the elderly widow on the other side of the room, shaking his head absently.] "It's just a tragedy, such a tragedy…"

Result: Ravishing Mourner, who had begun to feel more cheerful under the influence of wine and friendly conversation, is flung back into a state of severe depression. She excuses herself to see if the stable boy happens to have an extra horse tranquilizer.

Joe Six-Pack's Response

[Furrows his prominent brow in befuddled, misplaced umbrage.] "Jewish? Fuck that, I'm a fuckin' Christian, man!"

Result: Ravishing Mourner looks startled for a moment, then laughs out loud. "Jesus was a Jew," she says with good humor (news that Joe Six-Pack receives with speechless horror), then gracefully walks off in search of a more interesting conversation.

The G-Rogue's Response

[Nods his head with careful consideration, restraining a smile.] "My dear—and I say this with all due deference to the dearly departed—I may be a gentile, but I should be honored to undertake the responsibility of filling your hole."

Result: Sixty minutes later the gods look down smilingly, meditating on the sense of balance in the universe as they watch a ceremony of death punctuated in an upstairs bedroom by two individuals engaged in the rhythmic thrusts of life.

Situation #4

Our protagonist is a former army officer, who is wearing a dashing, if rather antiquated, suit. He stares out the window of a southern mansion in melancholic pain, contemplating the state of the universe after his Lovely Lass has cruelly wronged him for the last time. She bursts into the room and apologizes, but he curtly informs her that he's leaving her. "But where will I go? What will I do?" she implores with profound despair.

How does the southern ex-officer respond?

The Fancy Lad's Response

[Stern facial expression cracking, then collapsing into an arched-eyebrows expression of unctuous compassion.] "Oh, never mind, my darling, where there's a will, there's a way."

Result: Fancy Lad sets a new world record for cuckoldry, his conniving Lovely Lass subsequently cheating on him with 316 men, 68 women, one traveling circus, and one mammy.

Joe Six-Pack's Response

[Furrows his prominent brow in violent outrage, spittle upon his lip.] "Fuck you, you fuckin' whore!"

Result: In a stunning demonstration of Charm-Karma,

Joe Six-Pack is immediately afflicted with a debilitating case of erectile dysfunction, which persists until he breathes his final words (which, incidentally, turn out to be "Fuckin' A, man").

The G-Rogue's Response

[His face as stoic and inscrutable as Seneca's.] "Frankly, my dear, I don't give a damn."

Result: G-Rogue turns around, ignores the flushed, heaving bosom behind him, strides confidently away, and walks straight to the nearest brothel—where he sets a new world record for one-night amorous conquest that still stands today: 61 prostitutes, 88 neighborhood housewives, 115 neighborhood virgins, 19 neighborhood widows, one Sarah Bernhardt, one Mary Todd Lincoln, and one mammy.

G-ROGUE PROFILE:
JAMES BOND

Era: Possibly eternal, though currently twentieth- and twenty-first-century United Kingdom.

Appearance: Refined G-Rogue. Tuxedoes above all. Impeccably dressed, usually donning well-fitting formal attire tailored on Saville Row, custom-designed to conceal a holstered Walther PPK. Wears a white tuxedo under his snorkeling drysuit. Rolex or Omega wristwatch. Silver cigarette case. Many of his clothes and accessories are cleverly engineered gadgets or weapons. Carnation in the lapel.

Habitat: The world's finest hotels, casinos, driving recklessly in exotic sports cars, being held captive by villains, in bed with beautiful women.

Women: Women cannot say no to James Bond, even though he pushes their buttons and often rubs them the wrong way at first. However, while his forceful kisses are met with indignant resistance at first, the clenched-and-punching feminine fists always end up wrapped passionately around his back in the end. Enjoys multiple amorous escapades in each book or film, often motivated by patriotism. His sexual technique has the unusual side effect of making villainous women see the light of virtue and defect to the good guys. Prefers married women because it "keeps things simple."

Turn-ons: Women of all types ("as long as the collar and cuffs match"), fast cars, gadgets, a good tailor, England, vodka martinis (shaken not stirred).

Turn-offs: Sinister accents, homicidal orthodontics, Dom Perignon '53 at a temperature above thirty-eight degrees Fahrenheit.

Quote: "I've never killed a midget before, but there can always be a first time."

G-Rogue Credentials: The original international man of mystery, Commander Sir James Bond speaks many languages, has the most refined tastes, is skilled with hand-to-hand combat and every type of weaponry, and has a license to kill. Parents died when he was eleven, was expelled from Eton for mysterious reasons, went on to study at Fettes, Cambridge, Oxford, and University of Geneva. Bride murdered by his nemesis on their wedding day, causing enormous grief and thirst for revenge. Consumes a truly heroic volume of high-end alcohol and tobacco on a daily basis. Boasts an extensive knowledge of...everything. Perhaps the most erudite man on the planet, and certainly a preeminent authority on topics such as history, science, culture, women, and the bon vivant lifestyle. Has singlehandedly saved the world countless times, often while several vodka martinis are in his bloodstream. No matter how remote the location or adverse the conditions, has the uncanny ability to be having sex within two minutes of saving the world.

C. K. DEXTER HAVEN

Era: 1930s high-society Philadelphia.

Appearance: Refined G-Rogue. Splendid suits, neatly combed hair, ironic expressions, excellent posture, and an unmistakably patrician bearing. Also known to sport a bathrobe when entertaining unexpected guests in the wee small hours.

Habitat: C. K. Dexter Haven almost exclusively hangs out in the opulent mansion of his ex-wife's family—as an uninvited and largely unwanted guest prior to her marriage to her second husband. However, he is remarkably at ease in this seemingly uncomfortable situation, confidently inviting himself as well as total strangers to the nuptial events. Haven is also comfortable on his yacht, driving his luxury convertible, or in his bachelor pad surrounded by books, guns, and equestrian art.

Women: Monogamously in love with his ex-wife, whom he subjected to domestic violence in a past life and now merely subjects to his caustic wit. She can't stand his presence most of the time, but he somehow wins her affection back and impetuously marries her a second time, stealing her from her current fiancé on the day of their wedding.

Turn-ons: Sarcasm, feisty gingers, vessels that are yare, whiskey-and-whiskeys.

Turn-offs: Blackmailers, men who wear their hats indoors, phony Joe Six-Packs.

Quote: Antagonist: "Always the gentleman, eh?"
C.K. Dexter Haven [after a brief pause to consider the question]: "…Except on occasion…"

6-Rogue Credentials: Seemingly the perfect gentleman, Haven has a mysterious and scandalous past involving his ex-wife, a nasty divorce, domestic abuse, and a drinking problem ("she never had any understanding of my deep and gorgeous thirst"). His inscrutable code of honor leads him to get blackmailed trying to protect the family of his ex-wife who hates him. He is a master of mocking disdain, witty rejoinders, and sarcastic remarks, causing many a clenched fist in males and females alike. He uses "quite" as a complete sentence, is the original wedding crasher, and steals the object of his desire away from the arms of an ill-matched rival suitor.

APPEARANCE

While Gentleman Rogues may conform to more or less the same speech patterns, they are much more difficult to categorize with respect to physical appearance. As a G-Rogue can exist in any time, place, or realm of society, his appearance may vary accordingly.

That being said, when carefully examining all the factors involved in the equation of a Gentleman Rogue's appearance, some consistencies do start to emerge, and two distinct archetypes take shape. Most Gentleman Rogues may be classified as either

Note the threadbare wife-beater, the plebeian headwear, and the abominable grooming; you, my rustic friend, are no Refined G-Rogue.

a Refined G-Rogue or a Rugged G-Rogue. Essentially, it is a question of Posh Spice versus Scary Spice. (Although if you were to make such an analogy to a card-carrying Gentleman Rogue, he would likely quote Cervantes ["Comparisons are odious"] shortly before giving you the thrashing of your life.)

Both breeds share many of the same intrinsic qualities, and are equally allied in opposition to Joe Six-Pack, but they do differ in appearance. In this section we shall endeavor to scrutinize the taxonomy of these two subspecies and learn how to identify one from the other on sight.

THE REFINED G-ROGUE

Dress: Impeccably attired, a paragon of sartorial distinction. Typically donning formal wear, as it is perfectly acceptable to be overdressed if one is also overeducated. Tailored suits, tuxedoes, sports coats—the Refined G-Rogue will nearly always be found in a jacket, even if only a smoking jacket while he is enjoying a glass of brandy in his library prior to retiring for the evening (with his enemy's fiancée, perhaps). Tailored dress shirts.

Cufflinks. Full-length overcoats. Dress shoes, perhaps custom made by renowned cobbler Laszlo Vass. If he is found in a hat, it will be a dress hat. He will doff this hat to the ladies, and upon entering a room he will immediately take it off and hand it to a servant. *Avoids:* Shorts, T-shirts, wifebeaters, jerseys, athletic wear, excessively baggy clothing, low-slung pants, exposed undergarments, ripped jeans, skinny jeans, large belt buckles, flip-flops, baseball hats (particularly worn backward or slightly askew), bandanas, anything that says "No Fear."

G-ROGUE QUOTE:

"Leave the tight pants to the ladies. If I can count the coins in your pocket, you better use them to call a tailor."

—The Most Interesting Man in the World
(Dos Equis commercial)

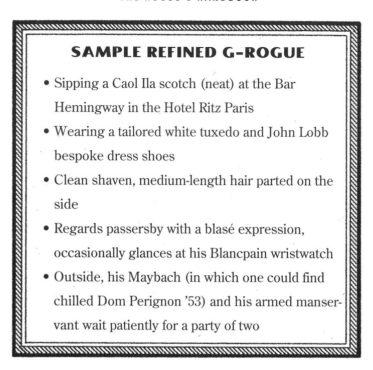

SAMPLE REFINED G-ROGUE

- Sipping a Caol Ila scotch (neat) at the Bar Hemingway in the Hotel Ritz Paris
- Wearing a tailored white tuxedo and John Lobb bespoke dress shoes
- Clean shaven, medium-length hair parted on the side
- Regards passersby with a blasé expression, occasionally glances at his Blancpain wristwatch
- Outside, his Maybach (in which one could find chilled Dom Perignon '53) and his armed manservant wait patiently for a party of two

Grooming: Clean cut. Neatly combed, medium-length hair. Usually clean shaven, although well-trimmed mustaches or beards are also acceptable. *Avoids:* Scruffiness, soul patches, chin-strap beards, mohawks, faux-hawks, dreadlocks, mutton chops, mullets.

Body Art: None—tattoos and piercings are emblems of the lower classes. One well-placed tattoo is occasionally

APPEARANCE

*The Aston Martin has long been a preferred means of transport
for the Refined G-Rogue.*

(but seldom) seen on the Refined G-Rogue, but only if it
is symbolic of something mysterious or extremely witty.
Avoids: Excessive tattooing, tattoos on the neck or hands,
Confederate flags, common/unimaginative themes, rural
themes, biker themes, violent themes, urban hoi polloi
themes, nudity, all piercings.

Accessories: Expensive but understated watches,
engraved money clips, engraved cigarette cases, engraved
lighters, spectacles, canes, long umbrellas, menservants.

Avoids: Gold chains, excessively gaudy jewelry, chains attaching the wallet to the belt, Bic lighters.

Posture/Expression: Perfect posture, ramrod back, graceful movements, blasé expressions, ironic expressions, subtle seductive grins. *Avoids:* Slouching; expressions of confusion, surprise, anger, or excessive zeal.

Conveyance: Chauffeur-driven limousines, foreign sports cars, foreign luxury cars, first-class trains, private jets, cruise ships, sailboats. *Avoids:* Coach class, pickup trucks, VW vans, big rigs, skateboards, buses, subways, or other means of public transport.

The Ritz in Paris: The hotel bar has been a favorite haunt of Refined G-Rogues since Georges the bartender was serving up fine à l'eau to the Lost Generation.

Habitat: Establishments that require a membership, hotel bars, fine dining venues, upscale casinos, private parties, balls, establishments with a dress code, "The Club," in bed with a beautiful woman. *Avoids:* Amusement parks, biker bars, dance clubs, raves, strip clubs.

The Drink in His Hand: Martinis, scotch, fine wines, champagne, brandy, port. *Avoids:* Forty-ounce malt beverages, box wine, Jägerbombs, mass-produced domestic light beers.

THE RUGGED G-ROGUE

Dress: Perhaps a little rough around the edges, but attired with an undeniable sense of style. Disheveled or dusty clothing, jeans, boots (preferably with spurs), cowboy hats, pirate clothing, outlaw clothing, blue-collar clothing, adventurer clothing. Hats cocked at a rakish, impudent angle. *Avoids:* Excessively formal attire, polos and khakis, popped collars, jean shorts.

Grooming: Often scruffy or donning some kind of facial hair. Moustache/beard combos. Hair typically tousled and long or else totally shaven. *Avoids:* Mullets, Prince Valiant haircuts, neatly parted hair, Hitler moustaches.

With the exception of the unfortunate murse, Indiana Jones has the Rugged G-Rogue look down to a T.

Body Art: May have tattoos, but they must represent very intelligent or esoteric themes. Ears may be pierced (especially if G-Rogue is a pirate). *Avoids:* Tattoos with rural or urban hoi polloi themes, pierced brows, pierced lips, pierced nipples.

Accessories: Weapons, flasks, women of ill repute. *Avoids:* Jewelry, pocket watches, murses, pince-nez.

Posture/Expression: Casual, confident posture. Tough, masculine stride. Challenging expressions, inscrutable expressions, suggestive grins, inappropriate stares. *Avoids:* Supplicating, pleading, or unctuous expressions. Any display marking a lack of confidence.

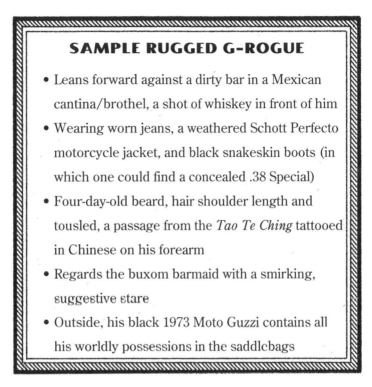

SAMPLE RUGGED G-ROGUE

- Leans forward against a dirty bar in a Mexican cantina/brothel, a shot of whiskey in front of him
- Wearing worn jeans, a weathered Schott Perfecto motorcycle jacket, and black snakeskin boots (in which one could find a concealed .38 Special)
- Four-day-old beard, hair shoulder length and tousled, a passage from the *Tao Te Ching* tattooed in Chinese on his forearm
- Regards the buxom barmaid with a smirking, suggestive stare
- Outside, his black 1973 Moto Guzzi contains all his worldly possessions in the saddlebags

Conveyance: Horses, motorcycles, classic muscle cars. *Avoids:* Segway scooters, roller blades, Mary Kay cars.

Habitat: Speakeasies, dive bars, saloons, cantinas, blues clubs, opium dens, burlesque houses, brothels. *Avoids:* frat parties, young professionals happy hour, '80s Night, Tupperware parties.

*The Rugged G-Rogue would likely give these overzealous frat boys
a wide berth lest he be tempted to waste the energy he planned on
spending at the brothel on giving them a thorough beating.*

The Drink in His Hand: Whiskey, absinthe, anything
drunk from a flask. *Avoids:* Appletinis, wine coolers, Smirnoff
Ice, drinks with umbrella garnishes.

PABLO PICASSO

Era: Twentieth-century France and Spain.

Appearance: Rugged G-Rogue, but not exceedingly so. Picasso conforms with the appearance standards less than the average Gentleman Rogue; he was too busy creating FIFTY THOUSAND works of art to devote too much time to his wardrobe. Loose-fitting trousers, sailor shirts, smocks. Certainly the balding virile type. His most notable physical characteristic may have been his piercing eyes, especially if he was looking at a woman. (He inhabited a world of symbols; perhaps the piercing quality was a metaphor.)

Habitat: Skipped class at art school to observe real life in cafés, brothels, and the Prado. Now he can be found in any halfway decent book about art, and in the best museums in the world.

Women: "There are only two types of women: goddesses and doormats." Famous/infamous for his oft inscrutable interactions with the fair sex, and for his octogenarian virility. Married twice. Sired three illegitimate children. Usually maintained several mistresses in addition to his wife or primary ladyfriend at the time. Most of his lovers were several decades his junior. At least two of his former lovers committed suicide after he died. The second time he married, it was for revenge. Upon being told by a girl he was chasing that he could do anything he wanted with her, a discombobulated Picasso replied: "That's disgusting. How do you expect me to seduce anyone under conditions like that? If you're not going to resist…well, then it's out of the question. I'll have to think it over."

Turn-ons: Girls at least one generation younger than himself (two if possible), shock value, Communism, himself.

Turn-offs: Formal education, Franco, Nazis, easy women.

Quote: "My mother said to me, 'If you are a soldier, you will become a general. If you are a monk, you will become the Pope.' Instead, I was a painter, and I became Picasso."

G-Rogue Credentials: After being admitted at a remarkably young age to Spain's greatest art school, he decided he hated formal education and dropped out. Became the biggest name in twentieth-century art, producing some fifty thousand works (many of which were scandalous), became one of the world's richest Communists. The tragic suicide of a friend caused him to paint in blue for three years. His revolutionary painting of a few whores shocked the world and established an art movement. First wife introduced him to 1920s Paris high society, but they were continually at odds because her sense of decorum conflicted with his innate roguishness. Questioned by the police under suspicion of stealing the *Mona Lisa*. Lots of very young mistresses, lots of illegitimate children. Viagra is nothing more than his essence in pill form.

G-ROGUE PROFILE:
RHETT BUTLER

Era: U.S. Civil War.

Appearance: Refined G-Rogue. Nineteenth-century southern aristocrat wardrobe, three-piece suits, cravats. Medium-length hair parted on the side, neatly trimmed moustache. Occasionally sports a top hat, which is courteously doffed to ladies as they pass. A knowing smile and a suggestive stare.

Habitat: Enjoying a life of leisure on southern plantations, playing cards in jailhouses (with his jailers), spiriting ladies out of burning towns in a horse and cart, spending quality time in brothels (and equally at ease in all of these scenarios).

Women: Passionately in love with one woman, Scarlett O'Hara (although he is "not a marrying man." Pursues her as a maiden, as a married woman (both times), and as a widow (both times). However, he shamelessly and confidently flirts with anything with a bosom, from radiant southern belles, to pious married women, to madams, to mammys. Master of the suggestive, inappropriate stare. "He looks as if…as if he knew what I look like without my shimmy…" Scarlett's attitudes toward Rhett initially run the gamut from indignation to hatred to harpy-like opportunism. Rhett sees all this and understands it, yet invites her to marry him

65

anyway—at which point her attitude becomes indifferent at best, bitchy and treacherous at worst. By the time she realizes she loves him, he had just made the determination that her bitchery and treachery would never end—so he calmly walks out on her, with the confident knowledge that there is another Lovely Lass out there somewhere worthy of his roguery.

Turn-ons: Bitchy women, gambling, brandy, impertinence, sarcasm, hopeless causes, women of ill repute.

Turn-offs: War, blind nationalism, propriety, effete rival suitors.

Quote: "Frankly, my dear, I don't give a damn."

G-Rogue Credentials: A chivalrous southern aristocrat, dapper appearance, articulate and well educated. Also a well-known blackguard, expelled from West Point, exhibits a fondness for drink. Was reportedly a professional gambler at one time, and was scarred in a knife fight. Very skilled with firearms ("one of the best shots in the country"), a daring blockade runner, overtly cynical but covertly idealistic ("I believe in Rhett Butler; he's the only cause I know."). Regular bordello visitor, legal guardian of prostitute's child, no decent family in his home town will receive him (including his own). Mysteriously wealthy, master of witty and inappropriate repartee, consistently notorious, scandalous, and talked about. "My dear, don't you know? That's Rhett Butler. He's from Charleston. He has the most terrible reputation."

4

PERSONALITY TRAITS

Although they do not enjoy conforming to much of anything else, the vast majority of Gentleman Rogues do share a host of universal personality traits. At the vanguard of this list are:

- Intelligence
- Civility
- Confidence

(And now abideth intelligence, civility, and confidence, these three; but the greatest of these is confidence.)

INTELLIGENCE

Intelligence is obvious—an almost prerequisite characteristic among heroes, protagonists, and persons of interest. One can hardly expect such an intriguing archetype as the G-Rogue to be deficient in this regard. But the intelligence of the Gentleman Rogue seldom manifests itself in the traditional way. The word "intelligence" traditionally calls to mind stodgy intellectuals, golden-boy valedictorians, and polite but socially inept chess champions. But the type of intelligence we're talking about—lurking with impertinence in the dark maze of the G-Rogue's cerebrum—can more accurately be described as a "sly cunning." Think Odysseus rather than Einstein (although it turns out ol' Albert did have a way with the ladies…perhaps he was something of a closet G-Rogue after all).

In any case, rather than the development of groundbreaking theories in physics, the cleverness of the G-Rogue is most often utilized for the sake of witty repartee, general mischief, and extricating himself from sundry quagmires. To find examples of the parries and thrusts of a Gentleman Rogue's wit, look no further than Rhett Butler, James Bond, Winston Churchill, Westley, Shakespeare's Mercutio, or TV's House.

Einstein's brain was perhaps his second most prodigious organ.

One hundred percent of G-Rogues will exhibit some degree of mischief, be it of a quasi-criminal variety (Robin Hood, Bob le Flambeur, Captain Jack Sparrow), or of an amorous type (James Bond, Lord Byron). And extrication? Dillinger's craftiness was beyond question when he orchestrated a jailbreak with a makeshift little wooden gun blackened with shoe polish.

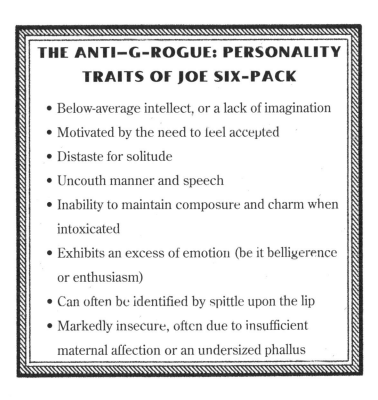

THE ANTI–G-ROGUE: PERSONALITY TRAITS OF JOE SIX-PACK

- Below-average intellect, or a lack of imagination
- Motivated by the need to feel accepted
- Distaste for solitude
- Uncouth manner and speech
- Inability to maintain composure and charm when intoxicated
- Exhibits an excess of emotion (be it belligerence or enthusiasm)
- Can often be identified by spittle upon the lip
- Markedly insecure, often due to insufficient maternal affection or an undersized phallus

These are but a few examples of the G-Rogue's mental keenness. But in all cases the most important and ubiquitous manifestation of the G-Rogue's intelligence is a sharp wit in conversation.

CIVILITY

As a gentleman, the G-Rogue will usually be a paragon of civility. (Remember, courtesy is one of the cardinal virtues of a chivalric knight.) However, what sets our mischievous protagonist apart from prissy and proper men is his habit of using his civility to cloak impropriety. Whether he is expressing sarcasm, insult, or blatant sexual impertinence, the Gentleman Rogue will deliver his message with the utmost civility. Consider 007's words in *The Man with the Golden Gun:*

James Bond: "Pistols at dawn? It's a little old-fashioned, isn't it?"

Bad Guy: "That it is. But it remains the only true test for a gentleman."

James Bond: "On that score, I doubt you qualify. However, I accept."

One may question the possibility of a civil insult, but the G-Rogue does not. It's all a question of delivery. When the situation demands affront, the Gentleman Rogue will not demean himself by resorting to a vulgar exchange. Foul language may be used on rare occasions, but in a matter-of-fact fashion—certainly avoiding any spittle-upon-the-lip, ill-bred excesses of emotion. The Gentleman Rogue's pride precludes any loss of control in this regard; he considers a lack of courtesy as symptomatic of the hoi polloi. As an example, following is a telegram exchange from the G-Rogue who said, "When you have to kill a man, it costs nothing to be polite":

G. B. Shaw: "Two tickets reserved for you, first night *Pygmalion*. Bring a friend...if you have one."

Churchill: "Cannot make first night. Please send tickets for the second night...if there is one."

The Gentleman Rogue also delights in obscuring totally inappropriate sexual innuendo with courteous language. But only he can pull this off with civility. To demonstrate this, consider potential innuendo responses from a G-Rogue and Joe Six-Pack to a lovely female coworker expressing discomfort and an inability to concentrate in the workplace:

Lovely Coworker: "I ran fifteen miles yesterday. My legs hurt so much I want to cry."

Joe Six-Pack: "That's fucked up; you should go home sick."

Lovely Coworker: "I ran fifteen miles yesterday. My legs hurt so much I want to cry."

G-Rogue: "Why, that's a pity, my dear. Shall I gently massage your thighs?"

CONFIDENCE

The Gentleman Rogue's sense of confidence is always positively overwhelming, sometimes bordering on bravado.

Scarlett: "I hate and despise you, Rhett Butler! And I'll hate and despise you till I die!"

Rhett [with unconquerable grin]: "Oh, no you won't, Scarlett, not that long."

The Gentleman Rogue knows, beyond a shadow of a doubt, that he will eventually prevail despite any adversity of the moment. Rhett knows that he'll get his girl (or else he's confident enough not to care). Every time that Milan Kundera's Tómas abruptly says, "Strip!" he knows very well that awkward, confused compliance is forthcoming. James Bond is captured and on the brink of death at some point in every one of his adventures, but those circumstances have little effect on his self-assured quips. Additionally, he knows instinctively that the girl who at first resists him as he forcefully presses his lips to hers will soon stop punching his chest and wrap her arms around his back—even if she's a lesbian (*Goldfinger*).

The G-Rogue isn't simply self-assured; he sweats confidence, it pours out of him with every breath, and that can

James Bond confidently knows that he can overcome any female foes if he can just get them on their backs (Goldfinger).

be a terribly magnetic attribute (except, of course, to the villains and rival suitors who are victimized by his confidence). Sir Winston Churchill boasted, "History will be kind to me, for I intend to write it." G-Rogue Pablo Picasso proclaimed, "Give me a museum and I will fill it." But Don Pablo didn't stop there; this bombastic Gentleman Rogue went so far as to paint the following scene from his childhood: "My mother said to me, 'If you are a soldier, you will become a general. If you are a monk, you will become the Pope.' Instead, I was a painter, and I became Picasso."

This attitude goes far beyond simple poise or pride—it is a borderline delusion of grandeur. Or it would be, rather, if the Gentleman Rogues in question didn't deliver. But they do—

Lovely Betrothed Young Lady: "I'm engaged, you know."

G-Rogue [amused]: "Is that right, my dear? And what do you suppose is the percentage probability that I'm going to steal you away from your gentleman friend? I'm going to estimate sixty percent."

Lovely Betrothed Young Lady [flustered]: "Umm…I don't know…I'm…I'm…I really don't know…"

G-Rogue: "Higher than sixty percent, I see. Seventy percent? Eighty percent? If it's higher than eighty percent, we can leave the soiree right now, you know—"

Lovely Betrothed Young Lady [meekly, halfheartedly]: "…he's a really good guy…"

G-Rogue: "I'm sure he is, but I'm better. Shall we?"

INDEPENDENCE

There is, in fact, a fourth trait as well, that of independence. And independence is a Gentleman Rogue personality trait so important that it merits its own chapter.

EL MARIACHI

Era: Turn of the twenty-first century Mexico.

Appearance: Rugged G-Rogue. "The biggest Mexican I've ever seen." Dark and mysterious: "…always walking in a shadow…as if the lights dimmed just for him." Dresses in black: a dusty black mariachi suit with a vague outline of a scorpion on the back, black boots with spurs. Tousled long hair, clean shaven or slight scruff, and a great mysterious scar on his hand.

Habitat: Within Mexico, anywhere the road to vengeance takes him, anywhere that poorly aimed bullets fly in his general direction, and anywhere that he can cause explosions that provide a fiery backdrop from which he can calmly walk away. Churches and confessional booths, seedy cantinas, within arm's reach of a murdered lover or friend.

Women: Gentleman Rogues often have a tragic romance lurking darkly in their past. El Mariachi has this in spades: not once, but twice did he witness the woman he loves murdered right in front of him, sending him into a spiral of grief and revenge. Often impertinent in dialogue with Carolina, and he also impressively manages to incorporate his spurs into lovemaking.

THE ROGUE'S HANDBOOK

Turn-ons: Guitars, guns, miscellaneous creative weaponry, revenge, women doomed to die.

Turn-offs: Illicit drugs, drug dealers, nefarious siblings, Danny Trejo.

Quote: El Mariachi: "Did I thank you?"
Lovely Lass: "No."
El Mariachi: "Okay. I will." [Exits.]

G-Rogue Credentials: Formerly a peace-loving mariachi, El Mariachi is a poster boy for The Mysterious, Tragic Past. No one even knows his name. When asked, "Who are you guys?" by the president, he vaguely replies, "Sons of Mexico!" Drug dealers killed the woman he loved, and then shot him through his hand—compelling him to give up a career in harmless guitar-playing in favor of a career in violent revenge, and forcing him to remember his murdered lover every time he looks at his scar. He falls in love again, but then a corrupt general slaughters his new woman and his child, forcing him to go on another rampage and kill a lot more scum-of-the-earth types. While dispatching hundreds of bad guys, he maintains a strict personal code—evincing a quiet religious sensibility, and spontaneously saving the president's life out of some nebulous sense of patriotism, morality, or constitutional justice. (Or, perhaps, just for the joy of a challenge.) And although he is perfectly okay with blowing away hundreds of baddies, illicit drugs he will not abide!

DENYS FINCH HATTON

Era: 1920s colonial East Africa.

Appearance: Rugged G-Rogue. Big game hunting clothes: lots of tan and khaki, wide-brimmed adventurer hat, tall safari boots, bullets in his vest and belt, usually seen toting a rifle. Finch Hatton is also an English aristocrat, and can pull off formal attire when the situation calls for it.

Habitat: The interesting thing about Finch Hatton is that he is a man with no home, no permanence, yet he seems at home everywhere. The fields and halls of Eton and Oxford, on safari blasting Mozart on his gramophone, romantically washing a Baroness's hair while reciting Coleridge to her, soaring above the African landscape in his airplane.

Women: At first Finch Hatton inspires irritation in the married Baroness von Blixen, and she refuses to even call him by his first name. But eventually she succumbs to the aura of mystery that surrounds him, and falls head over heels. He is fiercely independent, eschewing marriage or even spoken commitment. The first night they are together, she says, "If you say anything now, I'll believe it." He says nothing. The next day, during an awkward silence, she says, "I need to know how to think about this." His reply: "Why?" Later: "Doesn't it matter to you that I'm another man's wife?" "No. What matters to me is that you try so hard."

Turn-ons: Independence, the African wilderness, airplanes, poetry, Mozart.

Turn-offs: Domestication, colonization.

Quote: "I don't want to live someone else's idea of how to live. Don't ask me to do that. I don't want to find out one day that I'm at the end of someone else's life."

G-Rogue Credentials: Of noble background, son of an earl, educated at Eton and Oxford, but abandons it all for the freedom and open spaces of Africa. Always a solitary figure, as untamable as the Africa he loves, independence is a religion to him. A Renaissance Man, a poet-adventurer, exceedingly cultured, recites poetry and listens to classical music while hunting all sorts of beasts and saving baronesses from man-eating lions. Everyone loves him, but no one understands him. ("I've written about all the others, not because I loved them less, but because they were clearer.") He seems to like the animals more than people, and perhaps they understand each other better. After he died, lions started hanging out on his grave, ostensibly missing his company. "He was different from everyone else," his *London Times* obituary read. And he fairly and squarely steals a baroness away from a baron.

INDEPENDENCE

Jack Tanner: "Ann, I will not marry you. Do you hear?…"

Ann: "Well, if you don't want to be married, you needn't be…"

Jack Tanner: "But why me—me of all men? Marriage is to me apostasy, profanation of the sanctuary of my soul, violation of my manhood, sale of my birthright, shameful surrender, ignominious capitulation, acceptance of defeat… The young men will scorn me as one who has sold out; to the young women I, who have always been an enigma and a possibility, shall be merely somebody else's property."

—*Man and Superman*

Mothers, rest your nervous hearts: none of these fraternal lads risks growing up to be a Gentleman Rogue.

The G-Rogue is, essentially, a loner. A profound sense of independence is displayed in his every action and permeates to the core of his being.

One of the inherent mysteries of the G-Rogue is why he is as he is...what brought about this seeming infatuation with independence, what turned him into the lone wolf whose individualism is so intense that you can almost discern an intangible sense of melancholy and loneliness. The origin of

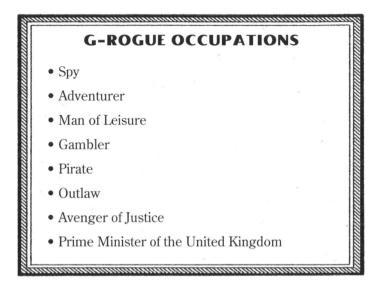

G-ROGUE OCCUPATIONS

- Spy
- Adventurer
- Man of Leisure
- Gambler
- Pirate
- Outlaw
- Avenger of Justice
- Prime Minister of the United Kingdom

his obsessive independence, like most other aspects of his personality, is shrouded in obscurity.

The Gentleman Rogue is not a team player. He is not an egalitarian member of any cohesive and synergistic unit striving for a common cause. He is not among the Super Friends. (He may have a sidekick or a helper on occasion, but even that is rare—he does his best work alone.)

James Bond provides a fine example. Yes, he is in the employ of the British government, ostensibly taking orders and working toward common, patriotic objectives. But 007 is always saving the world in solitary fashion:

M: "Remember, 007, you're on your own."

James Bond: "Well, thank you, sir. That's a great comfort."

—Octopussy

Occupational solitude is evidenced up and down the gamut of G-Rogues. Consider the *El Mariachi* series of Robert Rodriquez films: could there be a more solitary image than the lone mariachi walking down a desert road by himself, companionless save for a guitar case?

The G-Rogue's boot heels are well accustomed to the feeling of a lonely road (El Mariachi).

Or Captain Jack Sparrow, the pirate captain without a crew? Or *Casablanca's* Richard Blaine, with his perhaps-cynical, perhaps-not "I'm the only cause I'm interested in"?

The Gentleman Rogue may find collaborators, he may secure allies, he may even have a host of friends, but his vision and drive are marked by rugged individualism. The pursuit of his objectives is always single-minded and averse to compromise or committee. (If Ayn Rand's heroes had the slightest sense of humor or a modicum of devilish charm, they would make ideal Gentleman Rogues.)

BUT WHAT ABOUT THE LADIES?

The obvious extrapolation takes us to the G-Rogue's independence in the field of the fair sex.

Throughout the course of history, literature, and cinema, there might not be a single Gentleman Rogue who is a happily married family man. Many examples exist of the family man who was once a G-Rogue (Rhett Butler during his conjugal period) and of dastardly G-Rogues who leave their doting wives and adoring children (Shakespeare, Gauguin). There are also G-Rogues who are monogamously passionate but refuse to be tied down (*Out of Africa*'s Denys Finch Hatton). The only "family man" G-Rogues may be those who notoriously philander on the side (Lord Byron, Diego Rivera, JFK). Or some, like latter-day G-Rogue George Clooney, may simply have come to the sober and logical conclusion that matrimonial bliss is not something they wish to pursue.

Explanation? One is hard to determine.

The hunger for independence cannot be attributed to a fear of monogamy—perhaps the majority of Gentlemen Rogues are markedly single-minded in their devotion and pursuit of a particular leading lady (Rhett Butler, Denys Finch Hatton, Robin Hood, Zorro, Westley in *The Princess Bride,* etc., etc.). But when the G-Rogue attains the object of his desire, does he then sit back in his cushioned recliner, content, babies in his lap, and cease the sexually suggestive quips and all other gentleman roguery?

It is difficult to say. For the sake of storytelling and romantic tension, these tales seldom continue after the point when the female objective is realized. After the story ends, did Robin Hood engage in long weekend bouts of carousing with the boys, much to the chagrin of his bride, Marian? We know that matrimony did not tame the infernos of G-Rogue Diego Rivera, but was Zorro brooding and restless in the tidy and sensible home of Lolita? Did his eyes roam to new places in which to stick his rapier?

If so, we can speculate that gentleman roguery is a permanent condition and that G-Rogues are probably unsuited to the joys and burdens of domesticity, unless their partners display superhuman patience (Tereza in *The Unbearable Lightness of Being*) or equal roguishness (Frida Kahlo). If not, if Rhett could have happily bounced Bonnie on his lap from here to eternity, we might deduce that gentleman roguery is a mischievous phase in a man's life that can perhaps be overcome by the love of a good woman.

When asked what he hates most, Almásy replies, "Ownership. Being owned. When you leave you should forget me" (The English Patient).

But whichever the case, the G-Rogue—during the days that he is a G-Rogue—permits nary a string to be attached.

Bogart: "Walk around me. Go ahead, walk around me, clear around...Find anything?"

Bacall: "No, Steve, there are no strings tied to you. Not yet…"

—To Have and Have Not

YOU ARE NOT A G-ROGUE IF…

1. You respond well to authority
2. You seek the company of others more than they seek yours
3. You have to ask someone permission to go out

Unless he is wearing a disguise and kidnapping this family, the man on the right is not a Gentleman Rogue.

4. You have to call someone if you are running late
5. You call your mother more than once a week
6. You have ever said, "Thank you, sir, may I have another?"
7. You have ever purchased tampons
8. You have ever ridden in a sidecar
9. You have ever driven a minivan (unless you were in the process of stealing or commandeering it)
10. You have ever ridden a bicycle built for two
11. You are a member of the Boy Scouts
12. You adhere to any imposed rules prohibiting gentlemen's clubs
13. You know for certain how many children you have sired

THE G-ROGUE'S FAVORITE SONGS

1. "Solitary Man," Johnny Cash
2. "Better Off Without a Wife," Tom Waits
3. "Ramble On," Led Zeppelin
4. "It Ain't Me, Babe," Bob Dylan
5. "I Ain't Got No Home," Woody Guthrie
6. "Get Off My Cloud," The Rolling Stones

THE G-ROGUE'S LEAST FAVORITE SONGS

1. "With a Little Help from My Friends," The Beatles
2. "Don't Set Me Free," Ray Charles
3. "Stand by Me," Ben E. King
4. "We Are Family," Sister Sledge
5. "Wish You Were Here," Pink Floyd
6. "Who Let the Dogs Out," Baha Men (not because it has anything to do with independence, just because)

JAY GATSBY

Era: The Jazz Age—1920s Long Island and NYC.

Appearance: Refined G-Rogue. He has a man in England who sends him all manners of suits and dress clothes at the beginning of each season. Could be found in uniform in his younger, poorer days. Extraordinarily reassuring smile.

Habitat: Hosting parties in his sprawling, gaudy Long Island mansion. Cruising around in his gigantic luxury convertible. Lunching in fancy restaurants with notorious gangsters. Standing in his backyard, gazing forlornly at the green light across the bay.

Women: Gatsby spends most of his time trying to steal an old flame away from her current husband, who is very wealthy, of elite family, and a total douche bag. He focuses nearly all his energy on this task, making millions of dollars so he will be a more attractive suitor to her, and buying a mansion near hers and throwing outrageous parties with the hope she will wander in some day.

Turn-ons: Rich chicks, catch phrases, bootleg liquor, green lights.

Turn-offs: Being poor, the name Jimmy Gatz, douche-bag husbands.

Quote: Douche-bag Husband [spittle-upon-the-lip]: "I suppose the latest thing is to sit back and let Mr. Nobody from Nowhere make love to your wife. Well, if that's the idea you can count me out."

G-Rogue Credentials: One of Gatsby's singular characteristics is the aura of mystery that follows him everywhere. Everyone knows of him, everyone attends his parties, everyone talks about him. But no one really knows him or his story. Where did he come from? How did he manage to become such a fabulous millionaire at such a young age? Rumors abound. Did he kill a man? Was he a German spy? Was he in the army? Did he go to Oxford? Gatsby, for his part, fuels the fire of speculation, giving vague answers, misleading answers, fictional answers, or no answers at all. He employs an "elaborate formality of speech," Oxford manners, and refers to everyone as "old sport" (which is particularly maddening to his antagonists). The mystery around him obscures a shady past (and present), rife with bootlegging, gambling, and organized crime. He successfully (if briefly) steals away the object of his desire from her douche bag husband. But then he is blown away by a raging Joe Six-Pack.

RICK BLAINE

Era: World War II, French Morocco.

Appearance: Refined G-Rogue. White tuxedoes whenever possible. Otherwise, suits, trench coats, fedoras. Medium-length black hair slicked back. Constantly smoking cigarettes that are kept in a silver case in his inside jacket pocket. Also typically observed with a cocktail in his hand. Facial expressions usually convey cynicism, detached amusement, or nothing at all.

Habitat: The upscale nightclub/illegal casino he runs in Casablanca is the environment he is stuck with in the early days of World War II. But prior to that: born in New York, later seen helping the Ethiopians try to fight off the Italians, fighting against the Fascists in the Spanish Civil War, and making love to beautiful married women while sipping champagne in his beloved Paris.

Women: Historically indifferent to women, despite their feelings for him. ("He's the kind of man that…well, if I were a woman, and I weren't around—I should be in love with Rick.") Eventually encounters a married woman who causes him to lose his studied indifference. When she leaves him, he turns from idealist to bitter cynic and virtual nihilist overnight. But she returns…and when she does, she is prepared to trade in her incomparably noble and gentlemanly husband for the roguish Rick.

Turn-ons: Menservants that can play the piano, uttering iconic movie lines, the greater good.

Turn-offs: Vichy, Nazis, "As Time Goes By," hills of beans.

Quote: Ugarte: "You despise me, don't you?"
Rick: "If I gave you any thought, I probably would."

G-Rogue Credentials: Wrote the book on mysterious pasts—nobody knows why he can't return to America, or why he is such a bitter cynic now when he used to be an idealist and an activist. It was the perceived treachery of a woman that drove him to a philosophy of solipsistic nihilism. A married woman, that is—whom Rick could have easily stolen from her husband, but magnanimously decides not to out of regard for the fate of Europe and the free world. Often enjoys cocktails in contemplative solitude. Runs an illegal gambling den. Rigs roulette wheel to save the virtue of beautiful young bride, at his own personal expense. Is on the Nazis' blacklist. Has an extraordinarily protective and loyal piano-playing manservant. "He's a difficult customer, that Rick. No one ever knows what he'll do or why."

6

PERSONAL BACKGROUND

We shall devote but a few miserly lines to the subject of the Gentleman Rogue's background. Academically, it is true that G-Rogues the world over share a great deal of common ground in this particular area. However, discussion of this topic bears scant practical value if your wish is to cultivate yourself into a Gentleman Rogue, for there is little you may do to alter your past—except by resorting to mendacity, of course—but the *chevalier* lurking latently or blatantly in every G-Rogue will typically harbor a distaste for outright lies as an affront to his pride.

Put quite simply, the Gentleman Rogue almost always emerges from a mysterious past; his personal history is a series of shadows, a puzzle of nebulous parts. And a piece of the puzzle is usually missing. Every good G-Rogue needs a deep dark secret.

Athos of *The Three Musketeers* provides a fine example. While he does not frequently employ sexual innuendo and provocative witticisms as the ideal Gentleman Rogue would, he makes up for this deficiency with a sublimely mysterious past. No one knows why he is as he is—what event in his past produced such melancholy solitude, such romantic cynicism, and such excesses of wine. The genesis of his pseudonym is shrouded in the same tragic shadows that shape his temperament: his secret aristocratic background and his doomed marriage to the malevolent Milady.

El Zorro, like Timothy Burton's Batman or any other G-Rogue who sports a mask, also clearly has some secrets to maintain. And whisperings of Robin Hood's blue-blooded background encourage speculation, as do rumors of the origin of Captain Rhett Butler's wealth. Here, *Casablanca*'s Captain Renault attempts in vain to unravel the enigmatic past of Bogart's Rick:

A mask can be a very useful accessory for the G-Rogue who wishes to keep his background as obscure as his face.

Renault: "I have often speculated on why you don't return to America. Did you abscond with the church funds? Did you run off with a senator's wife? I like to think that you killed a man—it's the romantic in me."

Rick: "It was a combination of all three…"

Renault: "What in heaven's name brought you to Casablanca?"

Rick: "My health. I came to Casablanca for the waters."

Renault: "Waters? What waters? We're in the desert!"

Rick: "I was misinformed…"

As is perfectly common among G-Rogues, Rick is not particularly enthusiastic about the notion of shedding light upon the shadows of his past.

Bogart's character also displays a common motif among his ilk: the Gentleman Rogue's persona is often molded by some manner of tragic romance in his past. This misfortune can manifest itself in a number of ways: a simple broken heart (Rick), a doomed affair with a malicious woman (Athos), or a loved one who meets an untimely death at the hand of a villain (El Mariachi, James Bond). Although these events may have different effects on the G-Rogues in question (a solipsistic worldview, romantic cynicism, a taste for revenge), there can be little doubt that the affairs have left a profound stamp upon the character of the protagonist.

True G-Rogues prefer to quietly brood over their past with a bottle of liquor rather than discuss it (Casablanca).

YOUR OWN G-ROGUE PAST

But let us return to practical matters. If you wish to emerge from the shadows of your past as a Gentleman Rogue five years from now, by all means disappear for a while. Do your best to stumble upon some serious personal tragedy, a doomed love affair, and various other intensely metamorphosing events. With reckless, naïve abandon, pursue women who display signs of mental instability. Throw yourself body and soul into hopeless causes, refusing to let go until thorough disillusionment settles in. Keep the company of fascinating but shady individuals, such as spies, bullfighters, underworld figures, and prostitutes. Try to become embroiled in some unmentionably scandalous incident, and then move to a different city. But, most importantly, keep the circumstances of your intriguing past shrouded in secrecy (although certainly encourage speculation among well-wishers, adversaries, and, of course, curious young ladies).

If you wish to embark upon a career in gentleman roguery immediately, but you are not fortunate enough to have endured extensive—though nebulous—personal suffering, you have one alternative: merely develop an air of mystery about yourself. Answer direct questions with quotations and witticisms. Be rhetorically elusive. Tease your interlocutors with anecdotes and references that seem to be directed toward a moment in your past that will explain everything—then trail off with vagueness and a cunning smile. For example, here are some proper (and not-so-proper) approaches:

Curious Lady: "Where did you go to college?"
Joe Six-Pack: "Oh, I went to Penn State."

Curious Lady: "Where did you go to college?"
G-Rogue: "As Mark Twain said, my dear, 'I have never let my schooling interfere with my education.'"

Curious Lady: "Where are you from?"
Joe Six-Pack: "Oh, I'm from Dallas."

Curious Lady: "Where are you from?"
G-Rogue: "Where am I from? Hmm…Well, I suppose one could say I am citizen of the world."

Curious Lady: "What do you do?"

Joe Six-Pack: "Oh, I work for DHL."

Curious Lady: "What do you do?"

G-Rogue: "What do I *do*?"

Curious Lady: "Yes, what do you do for a living?"

G-Rogue: "Does it matter?"

Curious Lady: "I'm just curious."

G-Rogue: "Well, I do lots of things, my dear."

Curious Lady: "For example?"

G-Rogue: "When I'm not fighting in revolutions, curing various diseases, and saving babies from burning buildings, I suppose one could say I am entrenched in the intrigues of international commerce. Speaking of which, did you ever hear about J. Edgar Hoover's crusade against oral sex? In the end, he declared with profound disappointment, 'I regret to say that we of the FBI are powerless to act in cases of oral-genital intimacy, unless it has in some way obstructed inter-state commerce.'"

Curious Lady: "Oral-genital intimacy, eh?"

TIPS FOR ENGENDERING A MYSTERIOUS PAST

1. Avoid speaking of your past, but encourage speculation about it.

2. Be an orphan (or at least eliminate access to your family).

An ill-advised affair is one of the most effective ways an aspiring G-Rogue can achieve a tragic past.

3. Never live in the same city in which you grew up.

4. Create a large gap of time in your life during which no one knows what you were doing.

5. Experience a serious personal tragedy that changes you in a profound way.

6. Obtain a mysterious and visible scar.

7. Have considerable financial resources, but no obvious explanation of their origin.

8. Seek romantic liaisons that must be kept secret (they will end badly, which is desirable).

9. Seek scandalous company, such as spies, madams, and underworld figures.

10. Make cryptic remarks about your past when intoxicated.

G-ROGUE PROFILE:
LORD BYRON

Era: The Late Romantic Era, early nineteenth-century Britain.

Appearance: Refined G-Rogue. Wardrobe consistent with that of a nobleman. In spite of an unfortunate congenital foot deformity, was renowned for physical beauty and remarkable athleticism.

Habitat: Most comfortable in the boudoir of a married woman. Could be found at Cambridge as a young man, where he kept a bear in his lodgings for shock value. Witnessed in the House of Lords on occasion, and often seen drifting through European aristocratic social circles.

Women: By the time he died, Byron had made an amorous conquest of nearly every individual in Europe, regardless of age, marital status, social status, relation, or gender. Rumors of his truly heroic sexual résumé abound, starting with his own governess as a boy, and encompassing the most prominent female aristocrats of the time, maids, half-sisters, and every married woman in the known world. Perhaps the world's first case of celebrity stalking…A certain married Lady disapprovingly called him "mad, bad, and dangerous to know." She was obviously secretly fascinated, however, because she later carried on a scandalous affair with him—and when he broke it off she engaged in a long series of disturbing acts of infatuated stalking.

Turn-ons: Anything with a heartbeat.

Turn-offs: English bards, Scotch reviewers, early nineteenth-century British morality.

Quote: "Pleasure's a sin, and sometimes sin's a pleasure."

G-Rogue Credentials: An aristocrat, a poet, a lover, an adventurer, and a predecessor to the rock star. First book of poetry aptly named for a man of leisure: *Hours of Idleness*. Just like the Byronic Hero, he was an outcast, harbored an aversion for conformity to social norms, caused clenched fists in many a gentleman, and enjoyed some hardcore hubris. Racked up large debts due to his "reckless disregard for money." Regarded by many at the time as the greatest poet in the world, and also the biggest scoundrel. Sought self-imposed exile abroad when he tired of scandals in Britain. Most talked-about man in Europe—everyone loved to malign him, possibly because they were jealous that he wasn't sleeping with them anymore. Died fighting for the independence of a country not his own. Westminster Abbey refused his body due to his "questionable morality."

G-ROGUE PROFILE:
ZORRO

Era: Early 1800s colonial California.

Appearance: Ironically, Zorro's disguise is his maskless alter-ego, the all-too-refined Don Diego. Zorro masquerades as a passionless fop, a Fancy Lad. In reality, he is a Rugged G-Rogue: a masked brigand, dressed in black, sporting a wide-brimmed black gaucho hat, atop a rearing black horse, and brandishing a deadly rapier.

Habitat: Can be seen lounging in haciendas disguised as a Fancy Lad, hiding in chapels disguised as a priest, dueling with bad guys in fortresses, surreptitiously sneaking into the boudoir of his enemy's niece, or heroically poised on horseback, surrounded by cheering peons.

Women: Both the niece AND the wife of Zorro's enemy are in love with him after he successfully wins their respective affections from a rival suitor. The object of his desire is named Lolita, which now carries an undeniable sense of forbidden naughtiness in the post-Nabokov era.

Turn-ons: Social justice, swordplay, happy peasants, nymphets.

Turn-offs: Usurpers, Spaniards who speak with an English accent, oppression of the lower classes.

Quote: Zorro: "Do you surrender?"

Lovely Lass: "No, but I may scream."

Zorro: "I understand. Sometimes I have that effect."

(From the latter-day *Mask of Zorro*.)

G-Rogue Credentials: Nobleman by day, masked outlaw and hero of the poor by night, Zorro is very much the Robin Hood of colonial California. (So much so, he shares the same villain with Robin Hood—Basil Rathbone!) As with any masked hero, he is shrouded in mystery as dark as his wardrobe. Named "El Zorro" after the fox, as he uses his intelligence and cunning (and yes, perhaps his sword) rather than simply brute force. Manages to get both his enemy's niece and his enemy's wife to fall in love with him, effectively stealing them both away from a sinister rival suitor. Frequently inspires rival suitor to clench his fist in indignation. Kills rival suitor after goading him into a sword fight.

G-ROGUE PROFILE:
INDIANA JONES

Era: 1930's–40's (World War II and the years leading up to it).

Appearance: Indiana Jones is a Rugged G-Rogue: dusty adventurer hat, worn leather jacket, holstered pistol, long prehensile whip, nearly always unshaven, usually suffering from scratches, scrapes, and sundry wounds. His alter-ego Dr. Jones is a Refined G-Rogue: clean shaven, spectacles, dressed in tweeds or a tux, fond of bow ties.

Habitat: Wherever adventure (and preferably skeletons) can be found: jungles, deserts, evil temples where human sacrifice is performed, being held captive by bad guys, being chased by Nazis, etc.

Women: The lovely lasses that eventually fall for Jones are usually infuriated with him at some point, and are driven to slap or punch him. He engages in ill-advised sexual relations with a beautiful closet-Nazi (unfortunately shortly after his own father also enjoyed relations). Patented a brilliant pick-up move: from afar, lash your bullwhip around the girl's waist, then winch her in for a dramatic make-out.

Turn-ons: Biblical artifacts, feisty women, whips and chains, improbable escapes.

Turn-offs: Nazis, snakes, being referred to as "Junior."

G-ROGUE PROFILE

Quote: Lovely Lass: [immediately prior to what appears to be imminent coitus]: "I can be hard to handle."

Jones: "I've had worse."

Lovely Lass: "But you'll never have better."

Jones: "I don't know…as a scientist, I don't want to prejudice my experiment. I'll let you know in the morning."

G-Rogue Credentials: A gentleman and a scholar: University of Chicago educated, the world's foremost expert on archaeology, respected professor at a British university. Also a tough, wisecracking adventure seeker, he boasts exceptional fisticuff skills and marksmanship skills, and survives endless plots, ambushes, captures, and assassination attempts. Savior of destitute Indian villages and finder of lost children (while at the same time violating child labor laws by employing a small Asian boy as his loyal manservant). Frequently causes rivals to clench their fists with fury and exclaim, "Jones!"

7

THE MALE DYNAMIC

How does the Gentleman Rogue interact with other men? What roles does he play with respect to the masculine masses? What is their attitude toward him, and what is his attitude toward them?

Ugarte: "You despise me, don't you?"

Rick: "Well, if I gave you any thought, I probably would."

Casablanca

INDIFFERENCE

More than anything else, the G-Rogue typically regards other members of his gender with indifference. Of course, other attitudes may emerge depending on the situation and the roles being played. He may display any sentiment from bemused tolerance to mocking disdain. But a casual insouciance always seems to dwell under the surface. And, of course, we must keep in mind that the Gentleman Rogue regards a great many of the men he meets as potential rival suitors.

C. K. Dexter Haven (Cary Grant) of *The Philadelphia Story* provides us with a fine example. When dealing with Macaulay Connor (Jimmy Stewart), his sarcasm seems relatively light:

Macaulay: "Doggone it, C. K. Dexter Haven! Either I'm gonna sock you or you're gonna sock me!"

C. K. Dexter Haven [with bemused tolerance]: "Shall we toss a coin?"

However, when speaking to George Kittredge, rival for his ex-wife's affections, C. K. Dexter Haven's sarcasm is biting and antagonistic:

Like C. K. Dexter Haven (left), the G-Rogue should generally display an indifferent poise in the face of male antagonism.

Kittredge: "I have a feeling you had more to do with this than anyone!"

C. K. Dexter Haven [not even trying to conceal his disdain]: "Possibly, but you were a great help."

In both cases, however, you can see that Haven remains somewhat emotionally detached. Aspiring G-Rogues must nurture that sense of aloofness when encountering other males—be they gentlemen, rogues, or, most commonly, the omnipresent legions of Joe Six-Packs.

When presented with the antagonism of Joe Six-Pack, the G-Rogue has several avenues of acceptable response. He may express complete indifference to Joe's existence, he may display amusement, or he may respond with open disdain—but he must maintain a sense of civility, calm poise, confidence, and a general apathy to the entire encounter.

Consider the following scenario: A restaurant has been chartered for a private party. The soiree is in full swing when a man (G-Rogue or Wannabe?) walks in unaccompanied. He is immaculately attired in a white tuxedo. He regards the proceedings with a bored expression, until he notices the bar—and a particularly Lovely Lass at the bar. He walks over, orders a dry martini, turns to Lovely Lass, and the witty banter begins. But also standing at the bar (consuming

Jägermeister shots and mass-produced domestic light beer) is a hulking brute with a prominent brow. This particular Neanderthal, who is sporting jeans and a T-shirt, turns to the tuxedoed man with words of antagonism:

Joe Six-Pack: "What's with the fuckin' suit? Think that's gonna help you get laid tonight?"

Lovely Lass talking to Joe Six-Pack at the bar.

Unacceptable responses:

1. Wannabe G-Rogue #1 [stammering]: "Umm...no, not necessarily... I just thought...I just thought the attire would be more formal." [Lovely Lass, unimpressed and bored, walks off to seek someone with more interesting conversation to offer.]

2. Wannabe G-Rogue #2 [with gauche camaraderie, appealing to Joe's coarseness to gain his respect]: "Fuckin' A man, I hope so. Any decent tail here tonight?" [Lovely Lass, rolling her eyes with derision, walks off to seek someone with more interesting conversation to offer.]

3.   Wannabe G-Rogue #3 [glaring wrathfully, spittle upon lip]: "What the fuck do you care?" [Lovely Lass, unimpressed and slightly concerned about catching jackass germs from the spittle-upon-lip, walks off to seek someone with more interesting conversation to offer.]

Acceptable responses:

1.   G-Rogue #1 [with a blasé expression, as if his interlocutor did not exist]: "Quite." [Walks past Joe Six-Pack without a second glance. Lovely Lass stands there for a moment, then follows him.]

2.   G-Rogue #2 [laughing merrily, oblivious to the antagonism]: "Yes, yes, just came here from the governor's mansion, no time to change. Please don't ridicule me for the lipstick on the collar—that daughter of his is a wildcat!" [Lovely Lass flushes with embarrassment, but is undeniably intrigued nonetheless.]

3.   G-Rogue #3 [appearing inexpressibly bored by the whole scene]: "Well, like Oscar Wilde said, one can atone for being overdressed by also being overeducated—a conundrum you'll never be troubled with, no doubt." [Turns to Lovely Lass, extends a hand.] "Shall

we, my dear?" ["Yes, *mon ami,* I suppose I was fortunate enough to have engaged in a memorable amorous liaison yesterday evening."]

ENVY AND INDIGNATION

So do the masculine masses regard the Gentleman Rogue with the same indifference that he displays toward them? Not by a long shot. When 007 expresses confusion about why anyone would want to kill him, his boss sums it up perfectly:

James Bond: "Who'd want to put a contract on me?"

M: "Jealous husbands! Outraged chefs! Humiliated tailors! The list is endless!"

—*The Man with the Golden Gun*

The most common emotions that the Gentleman Rogue elicits from the rest of the masculine masses are indignation and perhaps a sort of competitive envy. Many of the men he encounters will become jealous, outraged, or humiliated before he leaves the room. They look at the G-Rogue as a dangerous, unpredictable animal that can cause injury to them in a number of ways (most significantly, by publicly embarrassing them with the sharp edge of his mocking wit—or by stealing their women).

G-ROGUE QUOTE:

Upon being asked by a rival what he could do that the rival could not do better, Lord Byron calmly replied, "Three things. First, I can hit with a pistol the keyhole of that door. Secondly, I can swim across that river to yonder point. And thirdly, I can give you a damned good thrashing."

Many members of the masculine masses will nervously avoid drawing-room conversations with Gentleman Rogues—especially if a conflict exists between them—as unnecessary risks. Contemporaries of Winston Churchill were probably terrified to engage him in conversation, for fear of a witty humiliation that would be quoted for decades. During the entire course of *The Philadelphia Story*, Kittredge is tangibly uncomfortable whenever C. K. Dexter Haven addresses him. Usually he snaps back with some ineffectual retort totally devoid of wit, but sometimes he just squirms in his skin ("You don't look as well as when I last saw you, Kittredge…Poor fellow, I know just how you feel!").

Husbands, fiancés, boyfriends, and rival suitors express their jealousy toward the Gentleman Rogue in a number of ways. *Out of Africa*'s Baron Blixen—always the gentleman—displays his righteous indignation to G-Rogue Denys Finch Hatton in such a civil manner that he seems only

G-Rogues often cause other males to clench their fists in indignation.

merely irritated by his wife's being stolen:

Baron Blixen: "You might have asked, Denys."

Denys: "I did. She said yes."

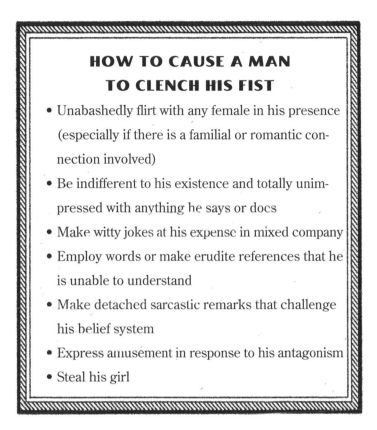

HOW TO CAUSE A MAN TO CLENCH HIS FIST

- Unabashedly flirt with any female in his presence (especially if there is a familial or romantic connection involved)
- Be indifferent to his existence and totally unimpressed with anything he says or does
- Make witty jokes at his expense in mixed company
- Employ words or make erudite references that he is unable to understand
- Make detached sarcastic remarks that challenge his belief system
- Express amusement in response to his antagonism
- Steal his girl

With that being said, most victimized husbands, fiancés, boyfriends, and rival suitors choose to convey their anger with either fisticuffs or some manner of nonviolent vengeance. Yet many rivals for a Lovely Lass's affections prefer to express themselves by attempting to murder the G-Rogue who is relieving them of their Lovely Lass. Sometimes they succeed (Tom Buchanan in *The Great Gatsby*); often they do not (Prince Humperdinck in *The Princess Bride*, Geoffrey Clifton in *The English Patient*). In any case, this is an occupational hazard that the aspiring G-Rogue must consider carefully before earnestly pursuing a career in gentleman roguery.

The masculine masses require no personal affront, however, in order to feel indignation toward the Gentleman Rogue. He is an affront to their entire society, an insult to propriety and the standards of acceptable behavior. (Plus, it is very likely that he once humiliated or stole a fiancée away from a close friend of theirs.) Often, it is not his actions

Classic Joe Six-Pack reaction to a G-Rogue: note the exaggerated emotion, the clenched fist, and the spittle upon the lip.

at all that inspire antipathy; it is simply his manner—the way he says things or the expression on his face. His antagonists seethe with anger when the G-Rogue employs sarcasm and will become even more upset when he regards their rage with equanimity or (much worse) amusement. Consider how a room full of indignant gentlemen responds to Rhett Butler when he questions the logic of going to war with the Yankees:

Indignant Gentleman #1 [irrationally upset by Rhett's cold logic]: "What difference does that make, sir, to a gentleman?"

Rhett Butler [with amused sarcasm]: "I'm afraid it's going to make a great deal of difference to a great many gentlemen, sir."

Indignant Gentleman #2 [grossly offended]: "Are you hinting, Mr. Butler, that the Yankees can lick us?"

Rhett Butler [calmly]: "No, I'm not hinting..." [Goes on to logically explain how the Yankees are much better equipped than the South.]

Indignant Gentleman #2 [irate, looking for a confrontation]: "I refuse to listen to any renegade talk!"

Rhett Butler [turns to #2, regards him with indifference]: "I'm sorry if the truth offends you."

Indignant Gentleman #2 [spittle upon lip, now hell-bent on instigating a duel]: "Apologies aren't enough, sir! I hear you were turned out of West Point, Mr. Rhett Butler. And that you aren't received by any decent family in Charleston! Not even your own!"

Rhett Butler [regards #2 with smirking amusement for a long, silent moment]: "I apologize again for all my shortcomings." [Bows sarcastically, turns around, and leaves the room after a few words to the host.]

Scarlett, who has been eavesdropping on the entire exchange, jumps back and conceals herself when Rhett exits the drawing room and walks outside. [Not shown: Scarlett's internal struggle: although part of her takes offense to Rhett's impertinent manner, another part of her is so overcome by his gentleman roguery that she wants to rush after him and beg him to gently relieve her of her virginity. But we shall explore this complicated subject of the female dynamic further in the next section.]

WESTLEY (AKA THE DREAD PIRATE ROBERTS, THE MAN IN BLACK)

Era: Feudal Europe.

Appearance: Rugged G-Rogue. Referred to by others as "The Man in Black." Black clothes, black boots, black mask. Longish, tousled hair; mustachioed. Carries a sword, with which he can overpower the most skilled swordsmen in the land. Known to appear very lethargic following resurrections.

Habitat: Aboard his pirate ship, scaling sheer mountain cliffs, or fighting vengeful Spaniards, simple-minded giants, and Lilliputian Sicilians. Braving the dangers of the Fire Swamp, enduring unspeakable torment in underground torture chambers, storming the castles of evil princes.

Women: Although Westley is monogamously passionate for Buttercup, he has no qualms about relentlessly nettling her. After he reveals his identity to her, he is playfully impertinent. But before that—when she only knew him as the Dread Pirate Roberts—he spends a great deal of time causing her to blush with indignation and clench her fists with fury. "You mock my pain!" she exclaims at one of his witty quips, shortly before pushing him down a hillside. Buttercup's responses reveal turbulent emotions beneath the surface; even if Westley had never revealed his true identity, she would have undoubtedly succumbed to the roguish charms of the Dread Pirate Roberts.

Turn-ons: Snobby women, Iocane powder, Johnny Cash.

Turn-offs: Faithless women, figures of authority, extraneous fingers, man-eating capybaras.

Quote: [Calmly observing Buttercup about to commit suicide via dagger to the heart] "There's a shortage of perfect breasts in the world; it would be a pity to damage yours."

6-Rogue Credentials: Wears a mask, dresses in black, has multiple identities, and is a bandit by trade. An air of mystery surrounds him. (Rival: "Who are you?" Man in Black: "No one of consequence.") Exhibits a healthy and innate opposition to authority. Extraordinarily courteous, even to adversaries. (After knocking his opponent unconscious: "Please understand I hold you in the highest respect.") Utterly refined in manner and speech, and his continuous witty rejoinders are delivered with an authentic English accent. Survives by his cunning—his vanquished foes recognize his unmatchable cleverness and seek him as a collaborator. ("I need The Man in Black...he bested you with strength...He bested me with steel. He must have out-thought Vizzini. And a man who can do that can plan my castle onslaught any day.") Also experienced miraculous resurrection.

G-ROGUE PROFILE:
LONE STARR

Era: Eerily similar to a long time ago, in a galaxy far, far away.

Appearance: Rugged G-Rogue. Appearance more or less consistent with that of Indiana Jones, minus the whip. Worn, dusty leather jacket. Cowboy boots, medium-length disheveled hair, slight facial scruff. Known to wear unfortunate Liberace-style outfits when attending royal wedding ceremonies.

Habitat: At the helm of his flying Winnebago, in his native Ford Galaxy, in the company of his faithful mawg, in pretty much any scene from *Star Wars*.

Women: Lone Starr doesn't exactly tirelessly pursue Princess Vespa with love-at-first-sight yearning. In fact, he exhibits a notable antipathy toward her high-maintenance ways at the beginning of their acquaintance, and doesn't seem to have any patience for her at all. For her part, the princess is constantly offended and indignant at Lone Starr's impertinence, roguishness, lack of deference for her pedigree, and general rough-around-the-edges appearance and manner. However, the constant blushing of her indignation only serves to warm her blood, and by the end of the film she is dying to trade in her docile fiancé for a more virile intergalactic cowboy.

Turn-ons: Drewish princesses, human-canine hybrid menservants, Uranus.

Turn-offs: Virgin alarms, matched luggage, edible gangsters, Spaceballs.

Quote: "Well, what have we got here? Will you look at her? Those flashing eyes, those flushed cheeks, those trembling lips… You know something, Princess? You are ugly when you're angry."

G-Rogue Credentials: Mysterious past: found on the doorstep of a monastery as a baby, with a mysterious medallion around his neck; eventually discovers as a grown man that he has been a blue-blooded prince the entire time. Attempts to steal a princess's royal virginity, but thwarted by a prude robot and labeled a sex fiend. Adept at laser swordplay. Practitioner of a secret mystical power (the Schwartz), which enables its initiates to use telekinesis to lift objects and inflict harm upon the testicles of others. Rescues a kidnapped princess, then saves her entire planet for an encore. Purloins said princess from her humdrum fiancé on their wedding day.

8

THE FEMALE DYNAMIC

And here we have it, a fundamental crux of the thesis: one of the distinguishing characteristics of the Gentleman Rogue's identity is the unique interplay between himself and the Lovely Lass.

We have been carefully studying the innate characteristics of this creature—so how do these traits and behaviors manifest themselves in his interaction with women? And, most interestingly, how do they respond to his singular manner? The elusive Gentleman Rogue is quite simple to spot in the wild. His relations with the female of the species are marked by three characteristics:

- Indifference
- Impertinence
- Blatant and unabashed sexual innuendo

INDIFFERENCE

Perhaps surprisingly, the Gentleman Rogue's attitude toward the world's ravishing women is oftentimes strikingly similar to his attitude toward the masculine masses: total indifference. This is of the utmost importance to any diligent student of gentleman roguery.

No, it is not necessarily a commendable trait. And no, it does not necessarily result in romantic success. However, it is not a calculated amorous strategy—it's merely an inherent character trait, an instinct. When a Gentleman Rogue encounters a Lovely Lass, nine times out of ten his mantra is: "Frankly, my dear, I don't give a damn." Let's take a closer look at that scene and what it tells us about the female dynamic.

Scarlett: "What are you doing?"

Rhett: "I'm leaving you, my dear."

Scarlett: "Please, take me with you!"

Rhett: "No. I'm through with everything here. I want peace. I want to see if somewhere there isn't something left in life with charm and grace. Do you know what I'm talking about?"

Scarlett: "No! I only know that I love you!"

Rhett: "That's your misfortune."

Scarlett: "Rhett! Rhett! Rhett! If you go…Where shall I go? What shall I do?"

Rhett: "Frankly, my dear, I don't give a damn."

Yes, Rhett's indifference in this scene is undeniably cruel and perhaps indefensible. But one cannot argue with the results: for the first time in the film, Scarlett realizes that she is in love with Rhett, and has been all along. Is it a bitterly ironic twist of fate that Rhett no longer wants Scarlett (or could there be a causal relationship with respect to his indifference?). This is an extreme example, perhaps atypical of the degree of apathy and at what point in the acquaintance it takes place, but it does provide us with a theme of indifference.

More commonly, the G-Rogue displays his "Frankly, my dear, I don't give a damn" manner at the beginning of the acquaintance. A unifying characteristic of Gentleman Rogues is that they almost always display (externally, at least) relative indifference toward ravishing women at their very first introduction. Examples abound in print and celluloid, such as Bogart in both *Casablanca* and *To Have and Have Not,* Count Almásy in *The English Patient,* Captain Jack Sparrow in *Pirates of the Caribbean,* and Jack Tanner in *Man and Superman. Gone with the Wind* can also provide us with a more textbook example of early-stage indifference:

Scarlett: "If you think I'll marry you just to pay for the bonnet, I won't."

Rhett: "Don't flatter yourself; I'm not a marrying man."

Scarlett: "Well, I won't kiss you for it, either." [Smiles coquettishly, closes her eyes, and looks up to be kissed.]

Rhett: "Open your eyes and look at me. No, I don't think I will kiss you."

Of course, a gentleman of less roguish instincts would have eagerly kissed Scarlett, heart palpitating and sweaty hand shaking, as she was the belle of the county and seemingly the prize catch of the entire state of Georgia. And she would have become immediately bored by his puerile enthusiasm—because it would have been the same sort of reaction she could have expected from any chump in Georgia. (But who is this enigmatic man who refuses to kiss her? Why, it's Captain Rhett Butler, Gentleman Rogue Extraordinaire! Why won't he kiss her? Who is he? What's so special about him that he doesn't want what every other man wants? Does he think he's too good for her?)

Although Gentleman Rogues presumably do not plan out their apathy beforehand as a tactic to bring about a desired amorous result, it is interesting to observe the effects of their behavior and speech upon the Lovely Lass. While G-Rogues universally exhibit initial

Non–G-Rogues showering Scarlett with overzealous attention and slavering enthusiasm.

indifference to comely vixens far and wide, the fair maidens in question also display somewhat consistent reactions.

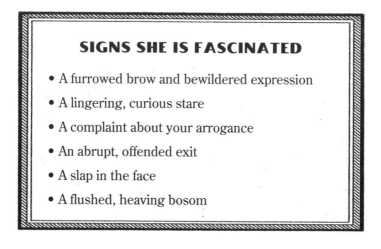

SIGNS SHE IS FASCINATED

- A furrowed brow and bewildered expression
- A lingering, curious stare
- A complaint about your arrogance
- An abrupt, offended exit
- A slap in the face
- A flushed, heaving bosom

It is important to note that a significant margin of error exists for the overall female response to indifference—but that margin interestingly becomes smaller and smaller as the test sample of lasses becomes more ravishing. By the time you get to the top fifth percentile of classical female beauty, the margin of error is negligible: nearly 100 percent experience confusion and fascination. (We include only those Lovely Lasses who also have an inquisitive mind;

those incapable of recognizing the difference between G-Rogue and Joe Six-Pack are of no interest to the aspiring Gentleman Rogue and were not surveyed.) The explanation is simple: the most beautiful women in the world are not accustomed to men acting indifferently toward them. They are used to compliments, overzealous attention, slavering enthusiasm, and unsophisticated pickup lines, yes. But when the G-Rogue displays apathy (or even better, rejection) to a ravishing maiden, the initial response is typically confusion or uncertainty—this is not what she is accustomed to experiencing at the hands of the Joe Six-Packs of the world. The best of the Lovely Lasses—the women that the G-Rogues of film and literature are typically after—will see in this peculiar demeanor *something different* and will secretly appreciate that long before they may understand it. But whether they value nonconformity or not, all of the Lovely Lasses are imbued with a sense of curiosity by the G-Rogue's inexplicably stoic indifference to their historically intimidating beauty. (Who the hell is this mystery man who isn't succumbing to my feminine charms?)

IMPERTINENCE

Jack Tanner of Shaw's *Man and Superman* obviously is not behaving indifferently toward the comely Ann in order to win her affections. His attitude with this much-sought-after young lady is not just apathetic, but often curt and even hostile. So does she pine for disinterested Jack, or for her other suitor, who never fails to shower her with compliments and constantly professes his undying love for her? After four scenes of callous indifference and even explicit rejections, Jack receives this objection from Ann:

"Why are you trying to fascinate me, Jack, if you don't want to marry me?"

Casablanca provides us with another example where the G-Rogue's indifference breeds fascination and even infatuation:

Yvonne: "Where were you last night?"

My dear, I know you'd like to sleep with me tonight, but I never make plans that far ahead.

Rick: "That's so long ago, I don't remember."

Yvonne: "Will I see you tonight?"

Rick: "I never make plans that far ahead."

Yvonne then attempts to get herself still more intoxicated in order to cope with her confusion and frustration, but Rick chivalrously/brusquely puts her in a cab and sends her home, in classic Gentleman Rogue antipodal fashion. His dialogue above actually pushes the envelope of indifference, bordering on antagonism or impertinence. And this brings us to the second key trait by which one can identify a Gentleman Rogue in his interactions with women: he pushes their buttons.

The G-Rogue almost always escalates his indifference toward the Lovely Lass to a playful sort of impertinence. He says things that should not be said, in such a way that she is not accustomed to being spoken to. He likes to get a rise out of her. All Gentleman Rogues in history, film, and litera ture have expressed their wit and their inappropriate sense of humor through impertinent remarks exchanged with the Lovely Lass. Some of the textbook examples:

From *Gone with the Wind*:

Scarlett: "Sir, you are no gentleman!"

Rhett: "And you, miss, are no lady."

Scarlett: "Oh!"

Rhett: "Don't think that I hold that against you. Ladies have never held any charm for me."

Scarlett: "First you take a low, common advantage of me, then you insult me!"

From *Out of Africa*:

Denys Finch Hatton: "Doesn't that outfit come with a rifle?"

Baroness Von Blixen: "It's…on my saddle."

Denys Finch Hatton: "Better keep it with you—your horse isn't much of a shot."

From *Out of Africa*:

Baroness Von Blixen: "Bror has asked me for a divorce. He found someone that he wants to marry. I just thought we might do that some day."

Denys Finch Hatton: "Divorce?"

From *The Princess Bride*:

Buttercup: "You're the Dread Pirate Roberts! Admit it!"

Westley: "With pride. [Bows.] What can I do for you?"

Buttercup: "You can die slowly, cut into a thousand pieces!"

Westley: "Tsk, tsk, tsk. Hardly complimentary, Your Highness. Why use your venom on me?"

Buttercup: "You killed my love."

Westley: "It's possible. I kill a lot of people…"

Buttercup: "…On the high seas your ship attacked. And the Dread Pirate Roberts never takes prisoners."

Westley: "I can't afford to make exceptions. Once word leaks out that a pirate has gone soft, people begin to disobey you, and then it's nothing but work, work, work all the time!"

Buttercup: "You mock my pain!"

From *Never Say Never Again*:

Ravishing Woman: "You know that making love to Fatima was the greatest pleasure of your life."

James Bond: "Well, to be perfectly honest, there was this girl in Philadelphia."

From *The Empire Strikes Back*:

Princess Leia: "Let go, please."

Han Solo: "Don't get excited."

Princess Leia: "Captain, being held by you isn't quite enough to get me excited."

Han Solo: "Sorry, sweetheart, I haven't got time for anything else."

From *Spaceballs*:

Lone Starr: "Well, what have we got here? Will you look at her? Those flashing eyes, those flushed cheeks, those trembling lips…You know something, Princess? You are *ugly* when you're angry."

From *Gone with the Wind*:

Rhett: "Tell me, Scarlett, do you never shrink from marrying men you don't love?"

Scarlett: "How did you ever get out of jail? Why didn't they hang you?"

As one can see from this last bit of dialogue, the immediate reaction of the Lovely Lass to the G-Rogue's impertinence is usually one of unconcealed frustration.

Bogart: "What made you so mad?"

Bacall: "I've been mad ever since I met you!"

Bogart: "Most people are."

—*To Have and Have Not*

Just as they are not accustomed to men regarding them with indifference, the most beautiful women of the world are typically not used to men making cheeky quips or antagonistic remarks at their expense. When the Gentleman Rogue begins to push her buttons, the general affront initially caused by his indifference becomes more personal, and her confusion blooms into frustration. (Why is he behaving like this? What does he have against me?)

Katherine: "Why did you hate me?"

Almásy: "What?"

Katherine: "Don't you know you drove everybody mad?"

—The English Patient

Of course, Count Almásy hardly hates Katherine—on the contrary, he is quite smitten with her. But his manner is pure Gentleman Rogue: indifferent and perhaps brusque. Katherine is certainly confused and frustrated by Almásy's manner, as any woman of her beauty, intelligence, and social graces would be. But underneath the confusion and frustration is an enormous fascination that metamorphoses into an undeniable and ultimately inescapable attraction. All of these feelings come to a head and explode into plain view during the scene where Katherine and Almásy finally give in to their passions. Wordlessly, Katherine walks up to Almásy and slaps his face, beating him with her fists again and again to give vent to her frustration. He stoically and wordlessly absorbs the blows—maintaining his air of mystery by not saying a thing—until she breaks down, runs her fingers through his hair, and asks him with her eyes to relieve her of her virtue. When the battle between frustration and fascination begins to rage in the mind of the Lovely Lass, fascination and attraction usually emerge victorious. This scene is the absolute archetype of the interplay between the Gentleman Rogue and the Lovely Lass, and variations of the scene often appear wherever G-Rogues are found.

BLATANT AND TOTALLY INAPPROPRIATE SEXUAL SUGGESTION

The third and final unifying characteristic with respect to the female dynamic is the Gentleman Rogue's propensity to engage in blatant and totally inappropriate sexual suggestion. Perhaps some primal courtship ritual ultimately lies beneath this behavior, but the most likely motivations for the G-Rogue are his need to exercise his sharp wit, his delight in pushing the Lovely Lass's buttons, and his general tendency to impropriety.

The Gentleman Rogue harbors a great love for the double-entendre. He has a suggestive quip for every occasion, and he employs sexual metaphors with smirking enthusiasm. Perhaps five percent of the remarks issued forth from the lovely lips of the Lovely Lass are ideal setups, lobs to the plate, opportunities for the G-Rogue to hit a ribald and roguish home run.

The gold standard for conversational sexual suggestion is James Bond—apprentice Gentleman Rogues would be well advised to carefully study the dialogue in these films. The G-Rogue must be able to think (lasciviously) on his feet and master the art of the quick repartee. A couple of examples:

Ravishing Woman: "I'll finish dressing."

James Bond: "Oh, please, don't, not on my account."
—Diamonds Are Forever

James Bond: "You're one of the most beautiful girls I've ever seen."

Ravishing Woman: "Thank you, but I think my mouth is too big."

James Bond: "No, it's just the right size. For me, that is."
—From Russia with Love

The reaction of the Lovely Lass to blatant sexual suggestion varies widely but typically falls into one of two categories. Many of the more proper maidens will blush at the impropriety and take offense. However, oftentimes the initial indignation will turn into curiosity—and perhaps a more interesting kind of curiosity than the sort that evolves from nonsexual impertinences. At the other end of the spectrum, some of the more spirited vixens will delight in the verbal foreplay and will enthusiastically participate in the suggestive banter of the G-Rogue:

Lovely Lass: "Would you like to come inside and meet my kitten?"

G-Rogue: "I should be delighted to meet your little pussy, my dear."

Lovely Lass: "Hmph. You're not afraid?"

G-Rogue: "Afraid?"

Lovely Lass: "That she might not…like you?…"

G-Rogue: "Quite the contrary, I'm sure she'll be putty in my hands."

Lovely Lass: "What makes you so sure?"

G-Rogue: "Because she's been locked up so long with nothing to do but…play with her little toys. She'll no doubt be quite excited to have me to play with."

Lovely Lass: "You're bad, aren't you?"

G-Rogue: "Not at all. Now, then, are you going to let me come inside?"

Lovely Lass: "You deserve to get scratched. After you…"

A STUDY IN PICTURES: REACTIONS OF THE LOVELY LASS TO THE GENTLEMAN ROGUE

Below are some of the most common reactions a Lovely Lass will exhibit when encountering the Gentleman Rogue. Some of them may display just one of these responses; others will demonstrate every single stage throughout the duration of their acquaintance.

THE ROGUE'S HANDBOOK

Shocked

Offended

Angry

Frustrated

Confused

Curious

Fascinated

COUNT ALMÁSY

Era: World War II—era North Africa.

Appearance: A Refined G-Rogue who is not afraid to go Rugged when the situation demands it. When in civilized society: tuxedoes and suits, neatly combed hair, clean shaven. When wandering around the harsh desert: unshaven, mussed and sandy hair, stylishly rugged attire. Later, bears an uncanny resemblance to Freddy Krueger.

Habitat: Exploring uncharted deserts, in bathtubs with beautiful married women, in his bachelor pad jamming to Hungarian folk music, carrying the injured woman he loves to the cave that will be her tomb while a soaring and emotive soundtrack plays, on his deathbed in abandoned Italian villas.

Women: Madly in love with the wife of a colleague (who turns out to be not a colleague, but a spy). He absolutely infuriates her at first, by being neither respectful of her marital status nor playfully flirtatious, but rather tersely and brusquely straightforward, an amorous bird of prey. She shows up at his place, gives him a vicious slap in the face, beats him furiously, then abruptly shifts gears and starts passionately running her fingers through his hair.

Turn-ons: Herodotus, cartography, sand, that place at the base of a woman's throat.

Turn-offs: Loquaciousness, ownership, homicidally jealous husbands.

Quote: "I once traveled with a terrific guide who was taking me to Faya. He didn't speak for nine hours. At the end of it he pointed at the horizon and said, 'Faya.' That was a good day."

G-Rogue Credentials: A man without a country. Almásy is a Hungarian count with a beautifully aristocratic European accent who forsakes castle and country to go adventurously gallivanting about the uncharted desert expanses of North Africa. Extraordinary sense of mystery, largely due to his aloofness and his insanely laconic speech ("You speak so many bloody languages, and you never want to talk"). Later, no one knows his name or nationality. Steals the wife away from a rather flavorless spy, carries on a passionate affair with her, and then suffers great torment when she breaks it off. The cuckolded husband eventually attempts to kill them all via kamikaze plane attack. Sells out to the Germans due to his own backward but strict personal moral code: he had made a promise that he had to keep. Inspired clenched fists in almost everyone he encountered: "Don't you know you drove everybody mad?"

HARRY MORGAN

Era: World War II French Caribbean.

Appearance: Sort of a Rugged G-Rogue with the capacity to clean up nice. Sailor's hat and coarse boating clothes much of the time, but then dons slacks and a blazer when back at the hotel grabbing a cocktail or bantering with beautiful stranded young women. Black hair slicked back. Cigarette usually in his mouth, sometimes lit by a beautiful woman.

Habitat: At the helm of his boat, fishing or smuggling members of the French resistance. In secret basements providing illicit health care to noble fugitives. In hotel rooms, being interrogated by the police, beating up the police, or engaging in witty banter with Lauren Bacall.

Women: Fond of a beautiful and somewhat distressingly mature twenty-two-year-old pickpocket (who is actually nineteen). Relatively indifferent at first, then remarkably adept at pushing her buttons. Lovely Lass: "You know Steve, sometimes you make me—" Harry. "I know; that's why I do it." Whether inspired by his indifference or something else, she gets over her infuriation with him and becomes hopelessly devoted, following him around everywhere, trying to take off his shoes for him, trying to draw him a nice hot bath, getting jealous of other women, etc. He bristles at this as an encroachment upon his independence, although she seems to take his independence as a challenge. "No, Steve, there are no strings tied to you. Not yet…"

Turn-ons: Distressingly mature teenage girls, lovable alcoholics.

Turn-offs: Violence toward women, picking on poor rummies, strings.

Quote: Harry: "What made you so mad?"
Lovely Lass: "I've been mad ever since I met you!"
Harry: "Most people are."

G-Rogue Credentials: Seemingly a cynical isolationist, Harry refuses to help the French resistance at first because it isn't worth it to him. (Vichy police thug: "What are your sympathies?" Harry: "Minding my own business.") Then he seems to help them strictly for the money… and yet he declines an offer from the police for ten times more money if he turns them in…No one really knows his background, what he's doing in Martinique, or why he does what he does. Skilled at blocking women's slaps and at extracting bullets. Wife of resistance leader goes gaga for him while her wounded husband is unconscious in the other room. When the husband wakes up he also goes gaga, stating that he wished he had Harry's bravery. Hates bullies, and stands up for ladies, helpless rummies, and wounded fugitives. Ends up unexpectedly joining the resistance, and when asked why, replies that he doesn't know.

9

THE NOBLE EIGHTFOLD PATH TO GENTLEMAN ROUGUERY

1. The Gentleman Rogue says "my dear" as much as possible.

2. The Gentleman Rogue defies social conventions and embraces outrageousness.

3. The Gentleman Rogue is a mystery of many parts and is always more interesting than his surroundings.

4. The Gentleman Rogue skillfully purloins Lovely Lasses from rival suitors.

5. The Gentleman Rogue is refined, courteous, and confident in speech and manner.

6. The Gentleman Rogue boasts a playfully impertinent sense of humor, employing sarcastic comments and blatant sexual innuendo with roguish abandon.

7. The Gentleman Rogue regards most individuals and situations with indifference or bemused tolerance.

8. The Gentleman Rogue is not afraid to exasperate or offend. Whither he goeth, the G-Rogue leaves clenched fists and flushed, heaving bosoms in his wake.

A flushed, heaving bosom.

THE MOST INTERESTING MAN IN THE WORLD

Era: Twentieth to twenty-first century, wherever Dos Equis is served and adventure can be found.

Appearance: By night: Refined G-Rogue. Preferred attire is a white shirt (loose and unbuttoned at the top) and a suit jacket. Also seen in black tuxedoes, white tuxedoes, suits, and smoking jackets. A thick, virile beard. Spends his days engaging in adventure, and will don whatever wardrobe is appropriate for that particular adventure (fencing gear, jai alai uniform, astronaut gear, marlin-fishing attire, samurai outfit, mountain-climbing gear, etc.). "Leave the tight pants to the ladies. If I can count the coins in your pocket, you better use them to call a tailor."

Habitat: Leisurely enjoying Dos Equis while seated at a banquette at an upscale club, surrounded by beautiful women. In his private quarters wearing a smoking jacket, a large bird of prey perched upon his arm. In a speedboat filled with beauty pageant winners. Surfing tidal waves. Landing in the ocean in a space capsule. Bathing in steamy hot springs with snow monkeys. Suspended by a rope on the side of a mountain, feeding baby condors.

Women: "His charm is so contagious, vaccines have been created for it." "The pheromones he secretes have been known to affect people miles away, in a slight, but measurable way." "He's a lover, not a fighter. But he's also a fighter, so don't get any ideas." On pick-up lines: "There is a time and place for them. The time is never. You can figure out the place on your own." Has avoided the public spotlight ever since his affair with the princess of Angola caused such a stir.

Turn-ons: Dos Equis (lager), feats of strength, facial hair, assisting animals in distress.

Turn-offs: Rollerblading, skinny jeans, modesty.

Quote: "I taught a horse to read my email for me."

G-Rogue Credentials: All the various qualities of a Gentleman Rogue essentially add up to one very simple, unifying concept: he is interesting. By virtue of his title alone, The Most Interesting Man in the World would likely qualify. Incredibly charming, always surrounded by beautiful women, extraordinarily skilled at pretty much everything, capable of performing amazing and exotic feats of strength (such as bench-pressing Asian nurses or arm-wrestling Communists), and the most worldly and experienced individual of all time ("His beard alone has experienced more than a lesser man's entire body") He is extraordinarily suave, dressing well and speaking with a great foreign accent, but at the same time he is a rugged man's man ("I fell in love with Dos Equis after my short stay in jail in Guadalajara"). "The police often question him just because they find him so interesting."

ERNEST HEMINGWAY

Era: Twentieth-century United States, Europe, Cuba, Africa, etc.

Appearance: Rugged G-Rogue. Tall and solidly built, with a thick, manly beard. Has been known to wear military uniforms, safari gear, or loose and comfortable clothes suited for drinking and fishing in the warm Caribbean climate. Typically seen with either a gun, a cocktail, or a pen in hand (or a combination thereof). Mysterious forehead scar that he refuses to explain.

Habitat: At his desk writing; on idealistic battlefields in Italy, Spain, or France; drinking absinthe in the cafés of Paris; running with the bulls and guzzling wine in Pamplona; marlin fishing on his boat off the coast of Cuba or Key West; hunting big game in Africa.

Women: Married four times and had innumerable affairs, constantly leaving one woman for the next. In the book *The Hemingway Women*, author Bernice Kert explains that Hemingway grew bored easily, and that "the conflict between his yearning to be looked after and his craving for excitement and freedom was never fully resolved."

Turn-ons: Cocktails, Paris, outdoorsman stuff, wars, bullfights, writing, adventure, boasting.

Turn-offs: Fascism, writer's block, eternal marital devotion.

Quote: Hemingway Character: "Drinking. Not just drinking. Drinking these double frozens without sugar. If you drank that many with sugar it would make you sick."

Kindly Whore: "And if anyone else drank that many without sugar they'd be dead."

G-Rogue Credentials: The original Most Interesting Man in the World. He was an unbelievable bastard, braggart, and boozehound, but was fascinatingly larger than life. Nobel Prize winner and one of the biggest influences on American literature. Participated in as many wars as he could. Carried a wounded comrade across a battlefield, when his own legs were torn apart by shrapnel and his knee shattered by a bullet. Also known to carry a drunken James Joyce home on occasion. Somehow convinced the government to subsidize his boozing and fishing in the Caribbean by claiming he was hunting German submarines. Was supposed to be covering the liberation of Paris as a reporter, instead spent his time joyously blowing up Nazis. The bar at the Hotel Ritz in Paris is named for him, after he supposedly liberated it from the Germans and promptly ordered fifty martinis. Survived numerous car and airplane crashes; was continuously courting death. The consummate man's man, but he was also a ladies' man—so don't get any ideas.

G-ROGUE PROFILE:
MIKHAIL PROKHOROV

Era: Twenty-first century Russia.

Appearance: Refined G-Rogue. Typically seen in high-dollar business suits. At 6'8", he towers over his business associates, friends, and the beautiful women that often surround him. Will don athletic wear when engaging in extreme sports, but will revert back to formal attire afterward. Closely cropped hair, mischievous smile.

Habitat: Boardrooms, mansions, on his 200-foot yacht, in Moscow's most exclusive nightclubs, in the world's most expensive house (which he backed out of purchasing, losing his $55,000,000 deposit).

Women: "Frankly speaking, I like women." Unapologetically surrounds himself with hordes of beautiful women. Arrested in France on suspicion of arranging prostitutes for his guests at a lavish party he was hosting. His response upon being released from jail: "The French elite is envious because they're lagging behind in fashion, in life, and in sex drive." When his sister was publicly insulted by a couple of miscreants, he declared: "Since I was a child I had a rule—to punish crudity and disrespect towards women.... If the two gentlemen...do not apologize to my sister in the next two weeks, I will do what every man should: I will personally beat the shit out of them. You know that I will."

Turn-ons: Beautiful girls by the bushel, the best food and wine money can buy, purchasing sports teams, adrenaline, minerals.

Turn-offs: Prudes, disrespect toward the fair sex.

Quote: "You cannot eat all food, you cannot drink all wine, you cannot have all women—but that's what you should strive for!" (An adage he recommends living by.)

G-Rogue Credentials: Richest man in Russia, a billionaire industrialist playboy who doesn't know (or seem to care) how much money he has. Raised among the Soviet elite, well educated in finance, became very proficient at bribery, largely owes his fortune to a rigged auction. Travels the world in a private jet teeming with Lovely Lasses. Skilled at kick-boxing and keeps assault rifles as toys. Enveloped with an aura of Cold War mystery, which he seems to encourage (even refusing to divulge his favorite color). Bought an NBA team for the fun of it. Bragged that spending time in a French jail was fun. Created an invitation-only social networking website called "Snob," which aims to connect members of the Russian elite classes who share a taste for the finer things.

10

TOP TEN ALL-TIME G-ROGUES

1. Rhett Butler, *Gone with the Wind* (Clark Gable)

Captain Rhett Butler: charming scoundrel, chivalrous blackguard, and above all, Gentleman Rogue. Even the most famous of G-Rogues falls short of the perfect archetype by one percentage or another; Rhett may be the only individual in print, celluloid, or history who conforms to the ideal 100 percent. He is the model, the quintessence, the baseline by which all other Gentleman Rogues are measured.

Taking a look at our definition of the term, he truly exhibits all of the contradictions and paradoxes with bipolar brilliance. He comes from good family, but his family won't receive him. At first he seems like the paragon of chivalry: he bows, he speaks with courtesy, he repatriates wedding rings to grieving, patriotic widows, etc. But then again, he also spends a truly heroic amount of time in the local whorehouse, is not averse to an overindulgence of brandy, and has been known to carry Scarlett off to his bed for a little nonconsensual sex (although, of course, she secretly wants him to). Rhett does conform to his own strange standard of honor a number of times, such as when he rushes off to fight in the war when it is already lost, but he is categorically unprincipled according to the other southern gentlemen of Georgia. Such gentlemen would surely testify that he represents an undesirable deviation from the standard, and Scarlett would be the first to describe him as "playfully mischievous."

One can read the chapter titles of this tome one by one and check off Rhett Butler's conformity to the G-Rogue standards. His speech: gentlemanly but roguish. Independence: "You haven't forgotten that I'm not a marrying man." His personality exudes intelligence, civility, and confidence. His background is replete with mystery. (Why won't his family receive him? Did he really make off with the Confederate treasury?) He regards the masculine masses with indifference, amusement, or disdain; his relations with the Lovely Lass are clearly marked by indifference, impertinence, and sexual suggestion. And, above all, he says "my dear" as much as humanly possible.

G-Rogue Quotient: 100%.

2. James Bond, 007 (preferably played by Sean Connery)

Bond is the clear choice for the number two spot on the all-time G-Rogue list. His only shortcoming is that he skews slightly to the side of gentleman.

Fewer individuals consider him a scoundrel than what we typically like to see in a G-Rogue, but his unrivaled accomplishments in the field of blatant sexual suggestion certainly make up for that. As such, he lives up to the ideal almost completely.

As with Rhett Butler, one can read through the chapter titles and check them off one by one with respect to 007. His speech is courteous, witty, and peppered with "my dears"; he demonstrates independence, intelligence, civility, and confidence; his background is suitably mysterious for his profession; he regards the masculine masses with indifference for the most part; and whether they be damsels in distress or femmes fatales, no Lovely Lass can withstand the onslaught of his double entendres and outrageous (yet composed) sexual suggestion.

G-Rogue Quotient: 98%.

3. Rick Blaine/Harry Morgan, *Casablanca/To Have and Have Not* (Humphrey Bogart)

Essentially, Bogart plays the exact same character in these two films, so we will lump them together to leave space on this list for another worthy Gentleman Rogue.

As with 007, Bogart is slightly less roguish than the ideal and lacking a bit in sexual impertinence. He lives up to the standard in all other G-Rogue qualities, however, and actually sets the benchmark for a few traits. His independence is

second to none ("no strings attached"), and his background is patently mysterious. His inscrutable personal code is beautifully G-Roguish—that oscillation from solipsistic ego-centrism to revolutionary acts provides the enigma that lies at the heart of any true Gentleman Rogue. Bogie's curiosity-inducing indifference to the Lovely Lass should also be carefully studied by aspiring Gentleman Rogues.

G-Rogue Quotient: 95%.

4. C. K. Dexter Haven, *The Philadelphia Story* (Cary Grant)

In many ways, C. K. Dexter Haven represents the perfect theoretical Gentleman Rogue. His speech, appearance, and manner are delightfully patrician, but are offset with jarring G-Roguish contradiction by his boozing past and his sustained impertinences.

His primary limitation is that his ignominious past remains in his past—he is now reformed, and, as such, fewer people consider him unprincipled as we generally like to see in a Gentleman Rogue. However, his repartee is witty, quick, and biting—inspiring indignation in both the masculine masses and the Lovely Lasses as well as anyone can. Also, let's not forget that he skillfully stole away his Lovely Lass from a rival suitor.

G-Rogue Quotient: 94%.

5. George Gordon, Lord Byron

Historical personages have a disadvantage relative to this study, in the fact that the image of their G-Roguery is less clear in our minds than the characters who have been con-

secrated to film or literature. Byron's life and works, however, have an indisputably cinematic character to them.

Some of his biographical elements are classical Gentleman Rogue paradoxes: he is a nobleman but an incorrigible reveler; a brilliant and accomplished man of letters yet keeps a bear in his attic and drinks out of a human skull for shock value; a family man but a philandering scoundrel of notorious and seemingly endless sexual successes.

The Byronic Hero, a literary archetype based on both his work and his biography, exemplifies some traits that are very interesting to our study: he is an outcast, outlaw, or loner; he harbors a distaste for social institutions, social norms, and propriety; he displays a disdain for gentlemen of authority or privilege; he is cynical and confident to the point of arrogance; he has a troubled or mysterious past. Sound familiar?

Byron had the antipodal nature of the Gentleman Rogue down pat—he was the nobleman who was "mad, bad, and dangerous to know." Con: his homosexual obsession with a clubfooted altar boy.

G-Rogue Quotient: 91%.

6. Count Almásy, *The English Patient* (Ralph Fiennes)

As a nobleman and a wife burglar, Almásy obviously lives up to both halves of the G-Rogue equation. In addition to displaying the gentlemanly manner and traits of the aristocracy, his profound independence contributes to his already apparent sense of mystery. ("What the hell made him leave his castle

and come out to the desert?" Katherine wonders with intense curiosity.) Finally, Almásy is extraordinarily successful at inspiring indignation in Lovely Lasses and the masculine masses alike. ("Don't you know you drove everybody mad?")

G-Rogue Quotient: 88%.

7. Denys Finch Hatton, *Out of Africa* (Robert Redford)

Finch Hatton is the paradigm of the Great White Hunter in Africa, a designation that carries with it an implicit sense of mystery. More often than not, Baroness Blixen is completely baffled by this enigma who listens to Mozart records while he's chasing down lions and tigers and bears. ("I've written

about all the others, not because I loved them less, but because they were clearer.") Denys also brings independence to an entirely new level, almost turning sol-

itude into a religion. In addition to his mysterious personal background and his extreme independence, his Oxford education and noble parentage (son of an earl) further qualify him for a spot in the upper echelons of the Gentleman Rogue pantheon.

Once again, his primary shortcoming is his reluctance to "let the rogue out" with the frequency and the degree of mischievous abandon that we like to see. Finch Hatton slays lions, quotes poetry, and fairly and squarely steals away the wives of barons.

G-Rogue Quotient: 87%.

8. Robin Hood

Like Almásy, the "King of outlaws and Prince of good fellows" provides us with another classical example of an individual clearly fulfilling the contradictory roles of the gentleman and the rogue.

Some traditions maintain that Robin Hood is a member of the aristocracy; be that the case or not, he certainly comports himself with a noble grace and uncompromising sense of chivalry. On the other hand, he is an outlaw, engaging in such illicit activities as poaching, robbery, and the bloody elimination of various baddies. Across the gamut of Robin Hood stories, our gallant outlaw lives up to the majority of G-Rogue attributes, although one could argue that he falls short in the realms of independence and the female dynamic.

G-Rogue Quotient: 86%.

9. Westley (aka The Dread Pirate Roberts, The Man in Black), *The Princess Bride* (Cary Elwes)

Who but a G-Rogue would react to the sight of a Lovely Lass on the brink of plunging a dagger in her heart with the words, "There's a shortage of perfect breasts in this world; it would be a pity to damage yours."

Much like Robin Hood, the Dread Pirate Roberts presents us with a noble outlaw. And although he is decidedly not numbered among the aristocracy, his gallant manner and

impeccable speech compensate nicely for his stable boy background. The Man in Black is shrouded with an air of mystery for most of

the film, and his keen wit—often manifested in impertinent remarks causing flushed, heaving bosoms in females and clenched fists in males—is an archetypal example of gentleman roguery.

G-Rogue Quotient: 85%.

10. Sir Winston Churchill

Sir Winston is probably not quite as dashing as we prefer our Gentleman Rogues to be, and he is certainly quite a bit chubbier. But what Churchill presents us with is a perfect model of what we like to see in an aging G-Rogue. He does

embody most of the requisite attributes being discussed: noble background (grandson of a duke and born in a palace); a sense of chivalry (a twentieth-century knight, for chrissakes); all the necessary personality traits, especially an indomitable confidence

("History will be kind to me, for I intend to write it"); and an unparalleled wit and inspirer of indignation. Insert his brain into the body of Johnny Depp or Errol Flynn, take a few classes in Totally Inappropriate Sexual Suggestion 101, and you have a Gentleman Rogue with a score of 100%.

G-Rogue Quotient: 82%.

Honorary Roguettes: Frida Kahlo, Mae West, Mrs. Robinson (*The Graduate*), Mata Hari, Amelia Earhart, Lady Brett Ashley (*The Sun Also Rises*), Tallulah Bankhead. (Note the absence of Sarah Palin.)

Rookies to Watch (twenty-first-century G-Rogues): Mikhail Prokhorov, George Clooney, Richard Branson, Sean Combs, Captain Jack Sparrow (*Pirates of the Caribbean*), Ironman, Daniel Craig's James Bond, Christian Bale's Batman, Dr. Gregory House (TV's *House*), Barney Stinson (TV's *How I Met Your Mother*), The Most Interesting Man in the World (Dos Equis commercials).

DIEGO RIVERA

Era: Twentieth-century Mexico.

Appearance: Rugged G-Rogue. Diego didn't exactly cut the svelte and noble figure; he was more of a Porthos—a gigantic dynamo of energy, passion, and revolutionary fervor (not to mention three hundred big fat pounds of sexuality). Overalls, smudged with paint, but will don a suit and tie when rubbing elbows with presidents or Rockefellers.

Habitat: In the middle of riots at art school, in Parisian avant-garde circles, at zealous Communist meetings, brawling with art critics, painting enormous revolutionary murals with a gun in one hand for protection from political enemies.

Women: All. Married four times, but the most notorious of philanderers. His seduction prowess is all the more impressive when one considers his portly, frog-like appearance. Married twenty-two-year-old Frida when he was forty-two, divorced her, then married her a second time for good measure. Some people may have heard that a fifteen-year-old Frida once confided to a friend that she desired to one day have Diego's child. What most people don't know is that every girl in Mexico confided the same thing to a friend at one point or another. But what no one knows for sure is how many of them really did usher his progeny into the world.

Turn-ons: Radical politics, creating controversy, setting the bar for Wilt Chamberlain, food, unibrows.

Turn-offs: Conventional notions of marriage and fidelity, the clergy, Rockefeller Center.

Quote: "Diego is not anybody's husband and never will be, but he is a great comrade." (Frida Kahlo)

G-Rogue Credentials: A revolutionary Communist descending from Spanish nobility, Diego was a contradiction in every way. Vilified by Americans and capitalists all over for his outspoken Commie ways, vilified by the Communists for making piles of money working for wealthy capitalists. Master of the tempestuous affair. Passionately devoted to Frida, but slept with everyone who crossed his path, including his wife's sister. Spent his formative years among the bohemians in Europe, painted murals with a pistol in his hand, personally convinced the president of Mexico to grant Trotsky asylum (after which the exiled revolutionary with a price on his head became his roommate). Had the testicular fortitude to paint a figure of Lenin on a mural for one of the biggest capitalists in the world, and then refused to remove the image upon Rockefeller's demand. Known to engage in fisticuffs with art critics. Ever colorful, controversial, and talked about, and fathered at least one illegitimate child.

DOC HOLLIDAY

Era: American Old West.

Appearance: Doc Holliday seems like a Rugged G-Rogue by today's standards, although he was exceedingly refined given the time and place. Always well dressed, typically in a black tailored suit with a cravat and a diamond stickpin. Big moustache, wide-brimmed gunfighter's hat. Carried a gun in a hip holster, another in a shoulder holster, and also packed a big knife.

Habitat: In his office practicing dentistry (as he coughed up his lungs over terrified supine patients), saloons and gambling halls across the Southwest, behind a six-gun, in the consumption sanatorium.

Women: His primary female companion may or may not have been a prostitute or madam at one time. She also may or may not have sprung him from jail in a dramatic rescue. We do know that there are not many women in his life—although he is dapper, good-looking, and refined, most fear either his occasionally nasty wit, his occasionally nasty weapons, or his always nasty hacking cough.

Turn-ons: Gambling, guns, whiskey, loyalty, big-nosed women.

Turn-offs: Clantons, McLaurys, Tubercles bacillus.

Quote: When asked if his conscience troubles him: "No, I coughed that up with my lungs years ago."

G-Rogue Credentials: Holliday is a southern gentleman, a professional gambler, and a dangerous gunfighter. Well educated and refined, knows the classic languages, cultured and witty, and a practicing dentist. Was more or less an outlaw, arrested close to twenty times—yet bizarrely, became best friends with the most famous lawman in the country after saving his life in a saloon standoff. Was a loner with few friends, but was always the first to saddle up and help Wyatt Earp when he needed an extra gun, and helped Earp track down and exact vengeance upon his brother's killers. Diagnosed with consumption and given just a few months to live, but lived fifteen more years, drinking copiously and living recklessly all the way. Fearless and indifferent to danger; may have had a death wish because he preferred to die on his feet rather than in a sana-torium. Killed a man for disrespecting a saloon girl. According to Earp: "Doc was a dentist…whom necessity had made a gambler; a gentle-man whom disease had made a frontier vagabond; a philosopher whom life had made a caustic wit; a long lean ash-blond fellow nearly dead with consumption, and at the same time the most skillful gambler and the nerviest, speediest, deadliest man with a six-gun that I ever knew." Also, his cousin Margaret Mitchell invented G-Rogue Extraordinaire Rhett Butler.

11

AM I A G-ROGUE?

Now that you've learned everything there is to know about being a Gentleman Rogue, the time has come to determine if you have what it take to join the elite group of G-Rogues. Answer the questions below as honestly as you can. At the end of the quiz is a key that will instruct you how to grade the quiz and determine whether or not you are a Gentleman Rogue.

1. What type of woman do you prefer?
   a. A blonde bombshell
   b. The exotic type
   c. A bookish preacher's daughter with midwestern values
   d. A buxom, scandalously dressed tart
   e. All of the above

2. What is your marital status?

    a. Happily married

    b. Unhappily married

    c. Cynically divorced

    d. Haven't met the right girl

    e. Mothers, lock up your daughters—I'm on the prowl

3. What type of clothing do you prefer?

    a. A tailored suit

    b. Jorts and a V-neck

    c. Well-worn jeans and a weathered leather jacket

    d. Low-slung, baggy pants and a wife-beater

    e. A polo and khakis

4. What type of hat do you prefer?

    a. Baseball cap worn frontward

    b. Baseball cap worn backward

    c. Baseball cap worn slightly askew

    d. Fedora

    e. Black cowboy hat pulled low over the eyes

5. What type of shoes do you prefer?
    a. High-end basketball sneakers
    b. Cowboy boots with spurs
    c. Penny loafers
    d. Bespoke brogues
    e. Flip-flops

6. What type of facial hair do you have?
    a. Clean shaven
    b. Scruff—I shave once a week
    c. Chin-strap beard
    d. Thick Grizzly Adams beard
    e. Soul patch

7. My preferred tobacco product is:
    a. Cuban cigars
    b. Chewing tobacco
    c. Hand-rolled cigarettes
    d. Sobranie cigarettes from an engraved silver case
    e. Marlboro Lights

8. My preferred vehicle is a:

    a. Vespa

    b. 1960s Triumph motorcycle

    c. Toyota Corolla

    d. Aston Martin

    e. New Ford Mustang with custom rims and custom exhaust

9. Where would you prefer to spend an evening?

    a. A disreputable saloon across the border

    b. A rave

    c. A frat party

    d. On the couch with a bong

    e. The bar at the Ritz

10. Which brand of beer do you prefer?

    a. Bud Light

    b. O'Doul's

    c. Mickey's Malt Beverage

    d. Maudite

    e. I don't always drink beer, but when I do, I prefer Dos Equis

11. Which kind of libation do you prefer?

    a. Piña Colada

    b. Franzia White Zinfandel

    c. Bourbon from a flask

    d. Dry gin martini

    e. Jägerbomb

12. If you had a dog, what would you name it?

    a. Max

    b. Princess

    c. Don Juan

    d. Tupac

    e. Cerberus

13. Which book do you prefer?

    a. *The Da Vinci Code* by Dan Brown

    b. *Memories of My Melancholy Whores* by Gabriel Garcia Marquez

    c. *He's Just Not That Into You* by Greg Behrendt and Liz Tuccillo

    d. *Tropic of Capricorn* by Henry Miller

    e. I don't read books

197

14. Which musician do you prefer?

    a. Frank Sinatra

    b. Dave Matthews

    c. Snoop Dogg

    d. Lou Reed

    e. Kenny Chesney

15. Which occupation most closely matches your own?

    a. Man of leisure

    b. Attorney

    c. Gambler

    d. Arena football player

    e. Plumber

16. Which sport do you prefer?

    a. Professional football

    b. Professional wrestling

    c. Figure skating

    d. Bullfighting

    e. Baccarat

17. Which vacation destination would you prefer?
    a. The French Riviera
    b. Daytona Beach
    c. Cancun
    d. The Super Bowl
    e. Kilimanjaro

18. Which superhero do you prefer?
    a. The Hulk
    b. Batman (Christian Bale version)
    c. The Green Lantern
    d. The Ambiguously Gay Duo
    e. I don't know a thing about this comic book bullshit

19. Which best describes your interests?
    a. Sports
    b. Music
    c. Politics
    d. Fashion
    e. Flushed, heaving bosoms

20. Which is your favorite hobby?

    a. Video games

    b. Reality television

    c. Carousing and philandering

    d. Tailgating and watching the big game

    e. Falconry

21. Which is your weapon of choice?

    a. A dagger concealed in your boot

    b. Semiautomatic handgun aimed sideways

    c. Pepper spray

    d. A scathing wit

    e. Your loyal manservant

22. If you had to get a tattoo, what would you have etched in your flesh?

    a. The name of a relative

    b. An eye in a triangle, emanating rays of light

    c. A naked female on a motorcycle

    d. The name of a prostitute you once impetuously loved

    e. Something with a Confederate flag theme

23. Which actor do you prefer?

    a. Paul Newman

    b. Andy Griffith

    c. Keanu Reeves

    d. Tom Cruise

    e. Jim Carrey

24. Which best describes your educational background?

    a. Four-year degree from a state school

    b. Valedictorian at Cal Tech, PhD from MIT

    c. Expelled from an Ivy League school

    d. Like Mark Twain, you have never let your schooling interfere with your education

    e. GED

25. What is a typical first date for you?

    a. Go to the movies and see a romantic comedy

    b. Two first-class tickets to Mexico City for dinner, fly back same night, explain that "You can't find decent *cochinita pibil* in the States."

    c. Dinner at TGI Friday's

d. Watch UFC at a sports bar

e. Breakfast the next morning

26. Which is your preferred method of birth control?

    a. Abstinence

    b. The withdrawal method

    c. Contraceptive sponge

    d. Vasectomy

    e. Not my problem

27. If you could have dinner with anyone, who would it be?

    a. Your significant other

    b. Jesus

    c. Michael Jordan

    d. Abraham Lincoln

    e. The girl next door who blushes when you look at her

28. If you found yourself in jail, what would most likely be the crime of which you were suspected?

    a. DUI

    b. Fine art heist

    c. Distribution of illicit substances

d. Pandering

e. Espionage

29. Where do you normally spend Thanksgiving?

a. At a parent or relative's house

b. You host friends and family at your place

c. Alternating European capitals

d. The buffet at Golden Corral

e. At a Mexican brothel

30. Have you ever had to sneak out of a woman's room to avoid getting caught by a third party?

a. Yes, in high school

b. Yes, in college

c. Yes, as a grown man

d. No, I haven't been in that situation

e. No, let them catch me, I don't give a damn

31. Has a woman ever left another (obviously less interesting) man for you?

a. No

b. Once

c. Twice

d. More than twice

e. A woman once left another (obviously less
   interesting) woman for me

32. Have you ever been confronted, threatened, or attacked
    by a jealous suitor, vengeful husband, or outraged
    brother for indiscretions with a Lovely Lass?
    a. Yes
    b. No

33. Have you ever been at a wedding where the bride
    looks back over her shoulder at you as she walks
    down the aisle?
    a. Yes
    b. No

34. How many times have you encountered a random child
    who uncannily shares your physical features?
    a. Never
    b. Once

c.   More than once

d.   I tend not to frequent establishments where children are permitted.

e.   I have very common features, so it's not unusual to encounter people who resemble me.

35. What would you do if a rival slapped you in the middle of a crowded formal soiree?

a.   Slap him back.

b.   Reply, "I beg your pardon, have I done something to offend you?"

c.   Laugh with genuine mirth, shaking your head in wonder as you turn around and walk away. On the way to the bar, still chuckling, make a signal to your menacing-looking manservant.

d.   Pull a Glock out of your belt and aim it sideways at his face.

e.   Calmly reply, "Your wife slaps harder than that, and I assume she's only playing. Shall we discuss this on the veranda?"

36. If a Not-So-Lovely Lass starts flirting with you at a bar, how would you respond?

   a. Blush crimson, speechlessly embarrassed that the beautiful people surrounding you might assume that the two of you are romantically linked

   b. Mutter, "Get lost, skank," and then turn to the bar and order a Bud Light

   c. Say, "In the words of Whitman, all women are my sisters or lovers, but you and I must avoid incestuous relations, my dear. Speaking of the latter category, why don't we invite your friends over there to join us?"

   d. Check your watch, magnanimously decide you are going to make this unfortunate soul the happiest girl on the planet tonight, stroll back into the bar (alone) thirty minutes before close, feeling proud that you had done a noble deed at great personal sacrifice

   e. Pound Jäger shots at the bar until the girl looks good enough to go home with

37. If your manservant asked you for a raise, how would you respond?

    a. Jump up from your chair and beat him with your riding whip.

    b. Politely hear him make his case, then motion to your other manservant to take him away.

    c. Gently refuse, explaining how in today's wintry economic climate, a manservant is a luxury you can barely afford.

    d. Inquire if he would be willing to take on the additional duty of keeping your lodgings well stocked with interesting young ladies skilled in conversation and equipped with bosoms of good potential; if he is, agree to a generous increase in wages.

    e. Hastily agree and suggest that the two of you immediately celebrate over a six-pack of Coors Light.

38. If your live-in lady friend were offered a lucrative job modeling and acting and asked you to move to Los Angeles with her, how would you respond?

    a. "Yes, ma'am!"

    b. Explain to her how she would not enjoy that

lifestyle, and persuade her to stay with you in your current city.

c. "Have fun in La-la land, my dear."

d. Negotiate for her to buy you a Maserati, then agree.

e. This is a trick question—I would not have a live-in lady friend.

39. You see an old flame at the wedding of a mutual acquaintance. As you amicably chat with her, you realize you are drawn to her more than ever before. Then someone congratulates her on her engagement. What do you do?

a. Nothing—she is obviously taken, and any move on your part would not be appropriate.

b. Say, "Don't do it. Come with me to Paris tomorrow."

c. Tell her she's a conniving tramp for flirting with you all night, then make some discreet inquiries as to her fiancé's identity and whereabouts.

d. Make a beeline to the bar and drink yourself into melancholy oblivion.

e. Say, "If it is really meant to be, you should be able to spend the night in my hotel room with me and a bottle of champagne and successfully resist any temptation. You owe it to yourself and your fiancé to be certain."

40. Consider this scenario proposed by Digital Underground: you're lying on your back with your head on the edge of the bed; the booty's two feet from your head. Should you:
    a. Take the time to find a condom
    b. You walk right over and you pound 'em
    c. You tell her that you want her love
    d. All of the above
    e. B & C only

Scoring: Apply the following points for each question according to your answer. Then add them up to determine if you are a Gentleman Rogue.

1) a = 0, b = 0, c = 0, d = 0, e = +1.
2) a = -1, b = 0, c = +1, d = 0, e = +1.
3) a = +1, b = 0, c = +1, d = 0, e = 0.
4) a = 0, b = 0, c = 0, d = +1, e = +1.
5) a = 0, b = +1, c = 0, d = +1, e = 0.

6) a = +1, b = +1, c = 0, d = 0, e = 0.

7) a = +1, b = 0, c = +1, d = +1, e = 0.

8) a = 0, b = +1, c = 0, d = +1, e = 0.

9) a = +1, b = 0, c = 0, d = 0, e = +1.

10) a = 0, b = 0, c = 0, d = +1, e = +1.

11) a = 0, b = 0, c = +1, d = +1, e = 0.

12) a = 0, b = -1, c = +1, d = 0, e = +1.

13) a = 0, b = +1, c = 0, d = +1, e = 0.

14) a = +1, b = 0, c = 0, d = +1, e = 0.

15) a = +1, b = 0, c = +1, d = 0, e = 0.

16) a = 0, b = 0, c = 0, d = +1, e = +1.

17) a = +1, b = 0, c = 0, d = 0, e = +1.

18) a = 0, b = +1, c = 0, d = 0, e = +1.

19) a = 0, b = 0, c = 0, d = 0, e = +1.

20) a = 0, b = 0, c = +1, d = 0, e = +1.

21) a = +1, b = 0, c = 0, d = +1, e = +1.

22) a = 0, b = +1, c = 0, d = +1, e = 0.

23) a = +1, b = 0, c = 0, d = 0, e = 0.

24) a = 0, b = 0, c = +1, d = +1, e = 0.

25) a = 0, b = +1, c = 0, d = 0, e = +1.

26) a = -1, b = 0, c = 0, d = 0, e = +1.

27) a = 0, b = 0, c = 0, d = 0, e = +1.

28) a = 0 b = +1, c = 0, d = 0, e = +1.

29) a = 0, b = 0, c = +1, d = 0, e = +1.

30) a = 0, b = 0, c = +1, d = -1, e = +1.

31) a = -1, b = 0, c = 0, d = +1, e = +1.

32) a = +1, b = 0.

33) a = +1, b = 0.

34) a = -1, b = 0, c = +1, d = +1, e = 0.

35) a = 0, b = 0, c = +1, d = 0, e = +1.

36) a = 0, b = 0, c = +1, d = +1, e = -1.

37) a = 0, b = +1, c = 0, d = +1, e = 0.

38) a = 0, b = 0, c = +1, d = 0, e = +1.

39) a = -1, b = +1, c = -1, d = 0, c – +1.

40) a = 0, b = 0, c = 0, d = +1, e = +1.

35–40: Mothers, lock up your daughters—you are a Gentleman Rogue Extraordinaire

30–35: A trifle roguish—a little effort and you could be causing clenched fists and flushed, heaving bosoms on a regular basis

20–30: Mainstream

< 20: You are either Joe Six-Pack or Fancy Lad

BOB LE FLAMBEUR

Era: 1950's Paris, Montmartre quarter.

Appearance: Unbelievably dapper, always wearing a suit or tuxedo, jacket always buttoned, tie always perfectly knotted, seldom a wrinkle. Pocket squares, the corners at perfectly crisp right angles. Trench coat. Neatly slicked hair, often wearing a fedora. Always smoking cigarettes voluminously. Poker-faced, narrowed eyes, never surprised. "A real hood's face."

Habitat: Seedy bars, nightclubs, cafés, surrounded by pimps, prostitutes, and hoodlums. Backroom smoke-filled gambling tables in "those moments between night and day." High-stakes casinos, either winning his fortune or losing it. Cruising around in his giant new convertible. In his large, two-story apartment, in which he keeps a slot machine in a closet and a woman of dubious moral character downstairs.

Women: Seemingly totally indifferent and positively imperturbable when presented with a beautiful woman. Plays the father figure, paternal and protective, a sagely guardian of girls heading in the wrong direction. One gets the impression that he is more interested in gambling, cocktails, and heists than he is in women. Still, at the end of the film the beautiful young girl is waiting alone in his apartment for him.

G-ROGUE PROFILE

Turn-ons: Gambling, gallantry, going to sleep after sunrise, charitable acts.

Turn-offs: Pimps, breaches of chivalry, bloodshed.

Quote: "I was born with an ace in my palm."

G-Rogue Credentials: Everyone knows Bob, and everyone admires him—from crooks to hookers to bartenders to cops. He is known as Bob the High Roller, and is a degenerate gambler. He is also a former criminal (he robbed a bank and did prison time) and a future one (he is planning a casino heist). Bob has a strange and strict moral code—he has no compunction with being a criminal, but maintains an absolute sense of gallantry at all times and strives to help those in need. Besides rescuing girls from prostitution, he takes the son of a dead friend under his wing, he loans a friend the money she needs to open a bar, he saves a cop's life. The cop likes Bob so much that he spends most of his time running around frantically trying to keep him out of trouble. He may be a criminal, but his personal code is strict—he doesn't use bullets during his robberies because he doesn't want to hurt anyone, and he hates pimps because they are an affront to chivalry. He slaps a girl for snitching on his heist, then leaves her his key so she won't have to sleep with someone to have a place to stay that night. Everyone looked up to that Bob le Flambeur "whose style was so cool, whose honor was so strong, whose gambling was so hopeless, that even the cops liked him" (Roger Ebert).

G-ROGUE PROFILE:
FIDEL CASTRO

Era: Twentieth-century Revolutionary Cuba.

Appearance: Rugged G-Rogue. A beard so virile and charismatic the CIA theorized he could be toppled from power if they could only find a way to remove it. Military garb topped off with a Comandante hat perched at a confident and authoritative angle. Cohiba cigar aggressively poised betwixt the lips.

Habitat: The mountains and jungles of revolutionary Cuba. On platforms making fiery speeches, flourishing a finger for emphasis. 99.9 percent of the time, his whereabouts are completely shrouded in mystery.

Women: The *New York Post* reports that a Cuban official named "Ramon" told a documentarian that Fidel has slept with a mind-boggling 35,000 women. Fidel's security team would allegedly comb the beaches of Cuba, seeking out the tastiest feminine morsels. "He slept with at least two women a day for more than four decades—one for lunch and one for supper. Sometimes he even ordered one for breakfast."

Turn-ons: Social equality, power, cigars.

Turn-offs: Yankee imperialists, capitalism, freedom of speech.

Quote: "If surviving assassination attempts was an Olympic event, I would win the gold medal."

G-Rogue Credentials: Son of a privileged family decides to give it up to become a guerilla leader, successfully toppling the government by age thirty-two. Tremendous sense of confidence (at his trial: "Condemn me. It does not matter. History will absolve me.") Transitions country into a Robin Hood government, robbing the rich to give to the poor. Inspires a tremendous number of clenched fists among the masculine masses, surviving a reported 638 assassination attempts. Has 9,700 menservants (his personal guard). While fighting the revolution, he took a brief break to father an illegitimate child with a married woman. The child grew up for years not realizing her parentage, but thinking that the most famous man in the country emerged from the jungle to bring all little girls gifts on their birthdays.

12

CONCLUSION

The G-Rogue life is not meant for everyone. The drawbacks associated with adopting a lifestyle of gentleman roguery are manifold and obvious—chief among these is the plain reality that the G-Rogue is not going to be winning any popularity contests. At best he will be regarded by others with suspicion; at worst he will be disliked, disparaged, exiled from certain social circles, and perhaps even find himself on the business end of a spittle-upon-the-lip Joe Six-Pack with an itchy trigger finger. Many will interpret his confidence as arrogance and his nonconformity as an insult. And, of course, his penchant for relieving rival suitors of their Lovely Lasses is unlikely to win him many supporters. We know that the Gentleman Rogue inspires other men to clench their fists in indignation—the aspiring G-Rogue would be well advised to remember that fists are often clenched as a prelude to a blow.

But the fact is, the true Gentleman Rogue could not care less if he is disliked, disparaged, or banished from good society. In fact, such reactions to his singular nature often inspire in him a certain detached amusement. The only thing that delights him more than the sight of a fist clenched in ridiculous indignation are the symptoms his scandalous nature inspire in the body of a lovely young lady.

The suspicion with which the G-Rogue is regarded is also worth investigating. What causes suspicion anyway? Confusion. We are suspicious of what we cannot understand. And generally speaking, there are two species of confusion: fear and fascination. Some individuals, male and female, will regard the Gentleman Rogue with a certain nervous fear. Others will regard him with a nervous fascination. In any case, the line is sufficiently blurry to permit traversing back and forth between categories.

Individuals studying gentleman roguery in order to obtain some esoteric knowledge in the field of seduction should probably turn their studies elsewhere. The G-Rogue inspires unadulterated love in the heart of the Lovely Lass far less often than he inspires some other emotions. Make no mistake: the Gentleman Rogue earns more slaps in the face than the rest of the masculine masses, be they Fancy Lads or Joe Six-Packs. But those fierce emotions that spring the slapping hand through the air can often belie other hidden or incipient passions, and the G-Rogue regards the sting of a slap with either detached amusement or Freudian interest.

Those who acknowledge and understand these sundry caveats and still wish to pursue a life of gentleman roguery now have the tools to do so. Study well the lessons herein, and you will always be the most fascinating person in any given room. People will talk about you often, although certainly not always in a positive light. People will look over their shoulders at you. Some of those glances will linger. You will regard it all with detached amusement.

A lovely lass glancing over her shoulder at you, Accredited Gentleman Rogue.

So now we know the characteristics and manner of the Gentleman Rogue back and forth—we know who he is and what he does. But have we unraveled the mystery of his motivation, *why* he is as he is? He is not in it for the girl, for the glory, or for the gold. He does not even seem to be in it for the fascination he arouses in others. Frankly, he doesn't give a damn. Perhaps he plays the game just for the sake of playing. In any case, his true motivation remains a mystery.

Lovely Lass [showing classic symptoms of agitation caused by a Gentleman Rogue]: "Why do you behave like that?"

G-Rogue [roguishly]: "Perhaps, my dear, I simply adore the sight of clenched fists and flushed, heaving bosoms…"